The Signs:

An Astrological Memoir

By

Sonja Marie

COVER PHOTO CREDS:

Lance Lamont – the late/great! We love and miss you brother!

Trina Fields – IG: 2myskies

Sonja Marie – Yet, another passion!

This book is dedicated to my countless

Angels, Ancestors, and Spirit Guides

that whisper powerful declarations

of strength, encouragement, and illuminating

"God Light" to assist and transform the lives

of my clients, my family and friends, and myself.

I am eternally grateful for your influence and guidance in this life,

past lives, and those in the future.

Contents

Acknowledgements

My highest appreciation belongs to God. Giving me the ability to see areas in our lives we need to highlight, give voice and ultimately heal. For instilling courage in me to use the modality of Western Astrology and translate it into a digestible meal for spiritual fortitude and internal wealth. I'm moved to tears every time I recall the reverence I have for Great Spirit. Thank you, Almighty Creator!

I am completely indebted to my mother, Celeste Spivey-Samuel, for raising me with a hard edge and sense of freedom. Encouraging me to celebrate my individuality by ushering me off to California, at 22 years-old, solo. "Show them what you're made of," echoes loudly in my subconscious. She has always been my biggest cheerleader; near and far. Thank you, Mommy for always giving me permission to fly!

A continuous wave of gratitude goes to my only offspring, Kamau. When I was chosen to be his mother, he quietly dared me to step into a higher calling for BOTH of us. He put a spotlight on my insecurities and mediocre ways of living and demanded I do more. Every day, Kamau reminds me to be my authentic self, in order to receive what I deserve. My son is my greatest source of inspiration.

Warm hugs of appreciation should be served to Anita Grant aka Mama Nit, for instilling countless hours of information and spiritual interpretation of Western Astrology. She fed my appetite for healing and self-reflection through a fun, honest and impactful understanding of our universe. In her words - "from my heart to yours" - thank you for openly sharing decades of knowledge with me.

I have been blessed to call many people, of all races, nationalities, sexual orientations and economics statuses, friend. They have paid my rent, invested in my projects, supported my musical ventures, wiped my tears, and have been the source of laughter until I peed my pants! Those I consider friends are my family. A special thanks must be extended to Lucy Taylor for investing in _The Signs: An Astrological Memoir_. Her time, words of encouragement and monetary support, honestly, made this composition a reality. When you have friends like her, impossible thoughts never exist.

I must extend a warm hug to all of my clients, social media supporters, and quiet prayer warriors I've never met. They understand how arduous my lifestyle can be; tapping into Spirit on command and extending my energy on *YouTube* when I had little to give. They are the Village we ALL need. Rooting for you from the bleachers, and silently championing your victory. I feel you constantly, and I couldn't be more grateful for your love.

A deep wave of appreciation goes out to my "tough as nails" Sagittarius writing coach, Kim O'Hara, founder of **A Story Inside Company**. Her honesty and guidance pierced through my Yonkers, NY disposition, and forced TWO books out of me in six months. She helped mold my words into a meal that could be desired by many. Thank you for seeing me through.

And I cannot forget my marketing guru, Lela Woodward, creator of *The Brand Lela Agency*. She walked into my life at a time when my intentions and talent were apparent, but my organization needed adjustment. Lela has a way of leading anyone out of entangling situations with grace, genius, and humor. I adore her dedication to all things "right for the community". She always sees the bigger picture.

And lastly, I want to thank ME for not giving up on the intentions of my soul while urging the unpopular decision of using astrology as a way of leading a life that assists many. Through it all, I have become my own best friend, and recognizing my light has given me permission to deliver my first book ever. If I didn't believe in myself, no one would.

Enjoy. Learn. Grow. Expand. Share…the words beyond this page. I thank YOU for being an integral part of my literary journey.

Foreword

My parents being hippies introduced me to the stars and their significance at a very young age. As a teenager, I started reading about my love life (or lack thereof) and checking dates that would help with my career. As an adult, I ventured out in getting full astrology readings. They were helpful, and usually accompanied by a lot of charts and symbols I did not understand. I always felt like a bit of a novice, and I knew there was something more. Something was missing.

When I met Sonja Marie, she was doing her incredible poetry and performing on stage everywhere. We discovered we were born on the same day, and our love for each other was instant. She always had a mysterious air about her, and the best mischievous smile in town.

When a close friend suggested I get a reading from her, I jumped at the chance.

We sat down, and I realized very quickly this was not going to be an average reading.

Sonja Marie spoke of dear family members that had passed on, that she couldn't possibly know the details of, with shocking accuracy. She shared wisdom that could only come from the ancestors. She is a true intuitive who incorporates the cosmos above and within. I found myself not only learning about how my life is in harmony with the stars, but also how to heal with their influence. I must mention her humor, for it comes in handy when dealing with painful experiences. She has a way of empowering you with her astrological interpretations; it will enable you to transform your life. I have come to her with my most vulnerable feelings, and never have I been let down.

Sonja Marie is unique, she is poetry, she is hip hop, she is magic.

She has earned and honed her gifts and is more than ready to share them with the world.

Cree Summer
Mama, Actress, Musician & Pirate Honey Brown

How to use "The Signs: An Astrological Memoir"

Western Astrology reaches far beyond the "just entertainment" factor, or fortune telling fun. In fact, the power of astrology to help us navigate our lives is extremely underestimated and devalued. When this modality is utilized in its fullest potential and limitless breadth of understanding, all energy existing in our universe is reflective. Fears, talents, and even your love languages are revealed, equipping us with information to evolve into our highest selves. Ultimately, once you commit to the teachings of the Signs, the knowledge and power are free. Shit, I'll take that over any overpriced vacation that promises to wipe away my superficial concerns! We beg to tune out, be less stressed, and quick fix our lives, but truthfully the answers lie in turning inward and discovering some hard solutions to the problems you are aware of subconsciously.

The Sun Sign, the sign most people focus on in a quick horoscope glance, serves as the core aspect of our personality; vulnerably shining specific intentions within ourselves, and throughout society. Yet, we have access to all of the signs as a means to navigate our day with awareness. Utilizing the knowledge of all twelve signs can influence how we communicate, how we initiate a project, and/or how we relate to children; just to name a few examples. Pure energy that insists – whether we are aware or not

- in guiding us throughout our present incarnation. What a pleasure to know the Signs and the Universe are here to make our lives better by asking us to pay attention to what is being told. Not through some un-reliable store front psychic, but by knowing you are your own seeker and knower of the truth.

The Signs: An Astrological Memoir highlights my twenty-year plus, explo-ration of the Sun Signs, reflecting through stories as they reveal specific characteristics of each zodiac constellation. I pray my understanding of the Sun Signs culminates my efforts in helping thousands of others down a path that ignites courage, faith, tenacity, acceptance, and drive. Just be-cause your Sun Sign isn't in Taurus doesn't mean you are unable to learn from the dependable, yet stubborn Taurian energy. Even though you may be a Libra, you can learn a lot from the decisive, forthrightness of Aries energy. Every Sign has a magical, yet spiritual intention to add value to our lives. It's powerfully used when we commit to the importance of its spiritual awareness.

Through humorous tales and life altering accounts, you will see how cer-tain Sun Sign energy has conveniently showed up to guide my steps. In an effort to share with you who I am, I've pinpointed how Sun Sign energy has unlocked stuck moments and inspired some specific life decisions. Try to find yourself in my stories; we are all but mere reflections of the great-ness God. And through our illustrious universe, He/She is eager to explain.

I've also integrated within each chapter, a specific account of the life of a male celebrity. As you read about artists, from Robin Williams to Prince, you may identify with similar attributes and behaviors, regardless of your personal opinion of their talent and public reputation. Take your time to connect with the similarities within your own life, and recognize we are born from the same universe with a similar song; we are one.

At the end of each chapter I thought to offer up a little advice in the voice of Archangel Haniel (at least the way I hear her). This beautiful Ascended Master is known for assisting all those who call on her via the art of communication; always timely, always in the Light of God. She is quick to recognize one's fullest potential and speaks life and joy through inspiring words and creative solutions to our challenges. Archangel Haniel poses as a direct line from earthlings to cosmic teachers flying high throughout our universe. In that way, she has a definitive connection and understanding of Western Astrology. As she dances among the stars, she gathers bite sized snacks of astrological interpretations for us to better ourselves and love unabashedly. We should never discount the power of Angels. They keep the world moving in a positive direction, long after human beings have given up.

The next time you take a walk around your neighborhood, consider a deeper meaning to what you see. Do you notice the resilience within the oak trees that line the street (Earth Sign Energy), or perhaps are lucky enough to witness the ease and pliability along the ocean's edge (Water Sign Energy)? Have you ever wondered what universal energy may fuel the patience of a kindergarten teacher, or what energetic surge elects itself as the match to ignite a social injustice riot for change (Fire Sign Energy, for sure)? Wherever you journey throughout your day, begin to consider the symbolism, its message and/or its purpose in our environment. We are blessed to be given representations of universal messages when we become more familiar with the positive and challenging aspects the twelve Sun Signs represent. They are integrated into all the components of the earth, both the practical and the magical unknown. My hope is to educate and assist with the healing of our lives through the awareness of Western Astrology, while simultaneously demolishing any myths created by religious control and the capitalistic greed of our modern civilization.

I invite you to utilize the information given in *The Signs: An Astrological Memoir* and answer the questions listed at the conclusion of each chapter to improve upon life, and better understand the purpose of each Sun Sign, commonly referred to as "energy". My aim to foster better relationships with our selves and others, while expanding your horizons with a sense of peace and surrender. Engage in the dance of God's perfection. Watch the constellations twinkle in symphony, creating healing songs that proudly sing your life's purpose. The universe is beyond considerate in this way: as above, so below!

CHAPTER ONE

───── ⌒⌒⌒⌒ ─────

ARIES – The Ultimate Risk

"I see you...exposed and dynamic and proud to be you!"

Everything starts with an idea. A dab of inspiration that provokes creation. Aries energy is the first reveal of human personality, according to Western Astrology; eager to burst into action and bushwhack outgrown concepts of life. This fire sign reminds the world to be on the constant hunt for new cycles in life, without a care in the world if it'll work or not. Aries is "the great risk taker". Lacking detailed knowledge or researched projections, Aries energy is presented throughout the world as a need to "shake up" confinements and allow the chips and the consequences to fall where they may. Akin to its earth bound representative, the Ram, it plows through any opposition that wishes to stand in its way. Headfirst and quite demonstrative, it threatens to rely on aggression if it doesn't get what it wants. Often equipped with brazen words and honest communication, those born to this sign believe life needs to be handled with authority in order to maximize our experience.

If you pay close attention, our society is marked with an array of Aries personality; the definitive act of war, the bodacious stance of riot and protest, and the bold initiation of startup companies risking billions of dollars that cater to the evolving technological need of millennials. This energy needs little permission to initiate change and progress. As a leader fostering tangible results, often times Aries pursues these dynamic missions alone, and like the magnetic energy of the pied piper; the rest of us will soon follow.

Bold. Forthright. Dynamic. Unyielding. Aries energy doesn't care what you think. If another disagrees with an Aries, they consider it a personal problem. Perhaps, the world holds a perspective born out of fear and a lack of ingenuity; that's not an Aries. They proudly march on, armored with confrontation and direct approaches. Although they may be challenged to finish a project - due to impatience and a lack of structure - according to them, launching a thought is key or nothing will be created. Aries energy prides itself on creating a movement justified by the needs of the community and screaming loud enough to wake up the masses. They solider for the underdog, the underprivileged, and the underappreciated, while searching for motives to disrupt the status quo. Aries energy must "keep it moving"! Boredom can lead to restlessness, which always brings them to a new cause. So, they are prone to take a nap periodically for recharging. Soon, Aries, the super nova of concentrated will, moves with an intensity that shuns maps, guides, and reasoning to get what it wants. Sheer volition decides the fate of any noble or small task; by any means necessary.

Aries energy is present within every person on the planet who dares to forge their own path. Regardless of your Sun Sign, this sustaining force helps us all to elevate and push forward into new arenas of life. Aries energy is indeed prevalent in my own life; periodically leading a life unfamiliar to most, but hellbent on solidifying the pioneer spirit within me. With that said, I've always been a true lover of words. The power they have to invoke feelings, understanding, joy, and insight. They produce endless hallways of colorful ribbons in my mind that bridge stories and outcomes, while creating landscapes my imagination is happily responsible for. As a teen-ager, reading the dictionary and playfully diving into a thesaurus were the best way to spend a Sunday afternoon. Prince, Stevie Wonder, and Michael Franks became mentors as they displayed crafty, sensual and meaningful ways of manipulating words and sound. My fascination led me to writing feverishly in my journals. Drowning in teenage breakup tears, painting the cold days of Yonkers, NY, and describing how my future would be shaped outside the constricting walls of my teenage hormonal indifference. Words still lift me out of my reality and place me into far away dimensions. It's a sacred dance I never want to end.

By the time I was in Los Angeles, and living on my own in my early twen-ties, I decided to find a way to establish "new life" for my love of words. The notion to fuse my poetry with music was spawned at a poetry read-ing at an infamous Ethiopian restaurant called Messob. Every Thursday night, music producers, actors, writers, and musicians would marvel at the creations laid out by beautiful literary artists. Even though history shows we've tunneled through the Beatnik era, and the well-known resurgence of The Last Poets and literary greats of the '60s, no one would think these poetry readings would initiate a part of my artistry that would garner me recognition for the rest of my life.

Oji Pierce, God rest his dynamic soul, was a prominent music producer sitting in the audience one night. Afterwards, he asked me if I've ever put my poetry to music, and I sheepishly responded, "No." He suggested we turn a crowd favorite, "When I Step", into a song which would feature a friend of mine, Kim Hill, singing the chorus. On a random, cloudless day in southern California, Kim, Oji, and I constructed a song that would turn my life around forever. I was amazed at the soulful conviction I displayed in words that represented the beauty and courage of Black women 'when we stepped'. I was blown away by the hypnotic melodies Kim crooned, and the punctuation of rhythm within Oji's production. I felt like the three of us took on an Aries conviction to push past the norm. Upon completing the first copy of our composition, a lane of artistic freedom opened up that only we belonged in. While everyone else was belting out young adult pleas for love and sex, we took a spoken word approach with music in order to speak confidence and pride by reciting deep, well-constructed thoughts, as opposed to singing them. I popped the cassette tape in my car and drove around for hours feeling simultaneously proud and frightened. Proud, because it was awesome to experience the impact our music had on those that heard it, but frightened because I knew there would be more who had no clue about this "modern day" expression. I felt different than most artists, and quickly began answering to the Aries-like surge bubbling throughout my soul. I forged a path that began to take on a life of its own. I'm so grateful I listened to that Aries, independent conviction within me. I took pride in explaining, "I'm not a signer, but a vocalist who rides a beat between the cadence of a rapper, and the hypnotic melodies of Sade." With this slight description, people who were unfamiliar with our sound were able to understand our creative direction. I wonder if they knew it was pushed by a foresight deeply present in my soul. And just like the Ram, I plowed through life making my influence felt with poetry and music, in my own way.

Aries energy has a raucous slant that is reminiscent of a child. Being the first sign of the zodiac, there's an insistence that hollers, "I am right, even if this is all I know. Accept it or move out the way!" It's sometimes an unruly identity, rooted in the right to be seen and heard even if they exaggerate a little (What? You've never heard of a little white lie?). Just smile and celebrate their gumption in all things, rather than shun them. You'll soon forget, as they find ways to "wow you" with countless, fearless attempts of exploration. How many times have you watched a child jump off a playground structure, only to cringe thinking they may hurt themselves? They do it again and again to achieve continued delight, while marveling at their own confidence for meeting danger only to win a small feat. We all can benefit from their self-absorbed need to find adventure at every turn and single handedly "go for it". We may think, "If the child survives, then maybe I will as well. Maybe, I'll blindly trust the will of God, and land where I'm supposed to." A child's jolt into existence forces them to handle whatever comes their way. Since they are draped in conviction, who will stop them?

I love watching Aries energy as it sets out on pursuits like a young spirit ready to seek and conquer, discover and rediscover, adapt or destroy in order to keep energy recycled and purposeful. You cannot promote happiness telling the same joke over and over again. However, it's so awesome to watch one adjust new information periodically, in order to propel interest with a fresh imagination. This approach may seem manic to some. However, it's pretty stimulating to the incarnation of Aries energy. Everything else seems confining, predictable, structured, and lackluster. Have you ever seen vibrancy in the eyes of a child living in a controlled environment? Of course not! They know true wonder is hidden in the exploration of the unknown.

Robin Williams always exhibited the varied amazement of life. The public was privileged to bear witness to this Aries trait he vulnerably expressed. As an actor and comedian, he flourished in a spontaneous world of characters and never-ending jokes, which celebrated the animated sides of his personality. He gave us permission to abandon the seriousness adulthood often brings. Through his many movies and television appearances, he reminded us to play with voices, costumes, and outcomes to humorous situations that seem to catch us by surprise. Turning a stand-up routine into a physical, acrobatic expression made us hold our breath, quite like a toddler jumping from a playground structure. He dared to push the boundaries of his own capabilities, just to witness a smile. He gave his all when he performed; saving nothing for later and steam rolling his creativity in your face, with a dab of Aries conviction that built excitement and wonder.

However, just like a child, he was ultimately unable to process what troubles he had lurking beneath a canopy of projected happiness. His childlike demeanor may have convinced him that "everything is going to be alright" even when, deep down, he felt quite the opposite. His untimely death may have left some wondering why someone wasn't aware of the trouble brewing within. However, I tend to think harping on that notion negates the joy he gave us, despite the sacrifice he experienced. The risk of leaning with intensity is a trait of Aries energy that we may take for granted. It rarely stops to think and process what the next step would be, only to enjoy the moment that's given. Mr. Williams will forever be admired for his jovial courage to turn our lives around with zany antics most comedians wouldn't attempt. He was known for being wacky, yet true to a vision of entertainment that the child in us is pleading to express. His adventurous spirit lives on, and when I think of him, I want to do a cartwheel, just because I can.

Aries people are generous like the ever-flowing fountain you may spot in the center of a town square. This sign has a forceful joyfulness that lacks concern about how to provide you with more of what you need. Interesting how someone so self-centered could be so open-hearted and bounteous. Maybe, it's because they give from a space of arrogance and ignorance. How dare you tell an Aries there's no more to give when the world is abundant, and they witnessed the imbalanced possessions some have over others! They act as a Robin Hood of sorts; robbing from the rich and giving to the poor, in order to achieve justice and rightful action. Aries energy snaps in, with a bold disposition, finding many ways to give so no one in their presence experiences a lack of time, money, or exuberance. The surge of this fire sign basks in the opportunity to lead any situation, as long as its followers are satisfied and content. You'll never hear them complain with petty interruptions. Aries energy knows it has a job to do, and they want to keep you happy while they do it. If you walk around your neighborhood grocery store and witness someone walking tall, chest out, with noble pride, I'll bet you just spotted an Aries.

Please note, their "puffed chest" may lead with ignorance. Aries people often times lack the desire to plan and exhibit preparedness. They may haphazardly give away money and belongings, in copious amounts, to keep life moving forward and seemingly running smoothly. According to the Ram, the particulars will hash themselves out later. There's a necessity needing to be fulfilled, and they are quicker than most to fulfill it. Someone else is capable of handling the follow through, as long as no one will be left in despair in the present moment. Aries energy will give from their hearts, wishing for nothing in return, because their independence internally secures any projected need. Aries energy shows up in the world as, "… fire in my belly, and a hustle for results in my heart. No one will ever be without!"

I often times subscribe to this Aries like insight of generosity when it's time to travel. I will drop everything to seize an opportunity to pack up and roll. Adventure and experience are priceless means to living a life fulfilled. Witnessing diverse cultures, drinking in the sarcasm of unfamiliar conversations and eating foods that shock my palate, are joys beyond description; a light beyond the Sun. Local destinations, staycations, and overseas excursions serve equal value. As long as every turn around a bend is something I've never seen before, I am enthralled and grateful for the opportunity.

I remember one weekend a few friends and I were itching for an escapade. None of us had children to be responsible for, spouses to report to, or standardized jobs we were locked into. We were free flowing artists, and we were broke. Twenty-something and curious, we were living amidst the beauty of southern California. So, we tapped into the roaming Aries energy we were all privy to, and ignorantly (but quite happily) we combined all of our resources to set out on an adventure we would never forget. All we knew was that we were going north to Big Sur, home of the beautiful, surreal redwood sequoia trees that literally resemble skyscrapers. I spent my last dime buying food for the five of us, providing extra camping gear and renting a big enough car for us to travel in comfortably. No one knew where we would end up, or what camp sites were available, we just wanted to add whatever we could to the experience. It was an exciting opportunity to join forces and marvel at the miracles of nature. We witnessed waterfalls that made our mouths drop open, we slept under trees that felt like protection in the middle of the night, and we sited cougars nursing their young. This act of rebellious generosity left us awe-inspired and full of wonder. The collective take-away was that the act of generosity is bigger than any material loss or the feeling of lack. It is the realization of what you gain, tangible or intangible, in any situation. That's the bountiful magic of Aries energy; it constantly gives, knowing there's so much more to be had. Be it ignorant or full of aggression, it's the joy and excitement of emptying a well only to fill it up again. Leading with the conviction that we will always be taken care of.

Maybe now, we will become more vigilant in a world that presents continuous opportunities to assert ourselves, lead with joy, and remain forthright in our steps while fighting for what's right. Aries energy is all around us, begging to begin something new and start our own trends. As scary as it may be for some, it's necessary in the spiral of evolution.

Questions for the Aries in you:

How do you generously add to your environment and/or the people around you, in order to aid their advancement?

How can you use your confidence to teach others the power of self and the importance of asserting their truth?

How often do you confront issues that highlight harsh truths others would rather ignore?

What's the best thing about being non-judgmental of others?

Haniel's corner:

Dear Aries, your frontline position leaves you open for attack and ridicule that most signs cower from. We rely on your strength to clear the way for God's miracles, which are not present in the vibration of the other eleven signs. Without you, no one can shine. However, remember that it's ok to harbor insecurities of your own, not knowing if a crazy idea will work, or if your lack of understanding will make you look uneducated or ill-informed. We all have internal pests that wish to shut down our purpose on the planet. Because you plowed through the course and unearthed hidden gems that would have remained unseen without you, lock into a quest to lead what's unpopular and watch respect follow. Being the first, you are necessary and true to this mission called life.

Mantra:

"I hold the vision many more need to see. I exercise patience in my crusade and respect the need for right timing!"

CHAPTER TWO

⎯⎯⎯ ❧⎯⎯⎯

TAURUS - The Manifester

"Enhancements to my existence - price tags swinging off my words -
possessions that come with false value mean nothing...if
I don't know my worth!"

Welcome to the second incarnation of the zodiac, Taurus energy. This is where our quality of life is looked at as an art form to obtain all we need, in order to carry out our life's mission. We are the gifts our Creator gave power to, in order to manifest what we desire. So, why is the majority of the world stuck in a poverty consciousness designed to tear us down and build us up, only to tear us down once again? Is it solely to dismantle our power to manifest? Every sign could benefit from Taurus energy if we learn to tap into its strength and fully believe in our personal power versus what society craftily deems important.

There's a subtle power in the Bull that's void in other signs. Taurus energy has a fierce respect for life that you can witness almost anywhere. I've noticed this energetic drive in the determined sincerity of special needs workers. How they carefully apply compassion and consideration in people less fortunate than themselves. The best magical position of this sign is to plow through difficult moments, rooted in the conviction of its earthbound shoes, while adding beauty and serenity wherever it lands. Most know that

Taurus energy is best noted for their stubborn disposition, leading with an understanding that life needs to evolve in quality, in order to live life fully. Although money is a constant conversation and a necessary tool, the purpose behind the green is what matters most. This sign recognizes the importance of having maximum options to create the best results. Luxury and opulence are not important. Its relationship "to have" supports the need "to build" a solid future. According to Taurus energy, one cannot exist without the other.

I read a quote once: "We are the only species on the planet that pays to live here!" We arrive from our mother's womb, securing an instant hospital bill that promises to keep us safe. We're conveniently placed in zip codes and school zones that tax our dollars and educate our children based on a viewpoint devised by Native Americans' betrayers. We're forced into jobs that squelch the human spirit and the imagination to make the 1% more money than they'll be able to spend in seventeen lifetimes. Taurus energy is a quiet ambassador on a mission to dismantle these confines. It marches in believing if one completely subscribes to these set visions, they will die decades before their heart stops. So, they methodically plan and protect their monetary investments and quality of life by envisioning themselves bigger than what the majority suggest they are. Taurus energy presents itself with a reverence that requires little validation. Their energy is present on the planet as a reminder that we are all worthy of the best. Whatever your sign, Taurus's prosperous nature screams, "Get yours!", hoping we all realize we are equally sacred as God's creations. So, why are we restricted when proving that notion to ourselves? Personally, I'm still searching for that answer. However, I've had several incidents in my life that helped me uncover how Taurus energy attempted to prove otherwise.

New York City in the '80s was everything! Hip-hop was an urban chemistry experiment about to explode, Republican politicians engaged in monetary orgies, and Gloria Vanderbilt Jeans were the shit. I had to have them! They were women's black or blue jeans that sported yellow stitching in the seam, ensuring a classic yet clean look. Gloria politely tagged a stylized signature on your right butt cheek, and a golden swan floated on the right front pocket for keepsake. They were a high waisted fit that gave every woman/girl the "booty cheek lift" we were searching for. At 14 years old, I felt tangible without permission and sexy without the knowledge of intercourse, but I wanted to be HOT! I burst into my mother's room one day, politely demanding she'd purchase me a pair. She must've had her cycle, or her current boyfriend was about to become an ex or maybe it was just Tuesday, but I didn't anticipate the barrage of questions I was about to receive. "How much do they cost? Why don't you ask your father? Do I look like a money tree? Don't you have some other jeans?" Let's be clear, my mom is a beautiful, generous, and hard-working woman, who collected a moderate salary and had wardrobe dreams of her own. She unleashed the importance of money and responsible spending on many occasions, but that day was different. Her response somehow targeted me viscerally and resulted in me feeling "less than". Celeste sounded like countless other single mothers monitoring their coins, but that mattered little. I needed Gloria Vanderbilt to validate me, lift my posterior, and make me shine. That day, I innately learned two worldly conditioning lessons: You ain't shit without Vanderbilt Jeans, and if you want them you have to get them yourself. The power of manifestation was born!

Gloria Vanderbilt was partly responsible for me recognizing the importance of abundance. I knew I had to look beyond my circumstances of living in

City Park projects, with moderate resources and a desire to look "fly". I convinced myself that I was already abundant and everything around me was already an inheritance, by nature. Like the birds that soar proudly in the sky and the fish who swim freely in blue waters, everything I want on this planet is mine. Tapping into Taurus energy will help everyone discover this to be true, as well.

So, I got a job and worked hard. I passed by Macy's Department Store every other day to scope my birthright on the mannequin in the window. I claimed those jeans, because I respected their position in my life. I learned to look past any material possession and notice the power we possess to manifest through planning, focus, and hard work. Society has been constructed to pigeon-hole most people; forcing us to rely on what's given to us, as opposed to how we can create a way. Taurus energy possesses a stubbornness that originates from its will to stop at nothing in order to obtain it's worth. It presents a powerful lesson to the world on how to vibrate higher and give attention to things that make you smile, righteously. The Bull teaches the world this concept through the conviction of loyalty.

Devotion is key to those aware of this Sun Sign energy. They display this clearly by almost always keeping their word to anyone that experiences them - their spouse, their children, a neighbor and/or a boss. You can bet your last twenty dollars if this earth signs says it will do something; they are hellbent to deliver! Taurus energy believes, in the midst of an ever-changing world, what you declare should be reliable and integral in upholding an honest trustworthy character. According to this sign, lies and deception have a tendency of creating complex problems Taurus people wish not to detangle. As we meander throughout the planet and spot an opportunity to live this simplistic way of life, you have the vibration of Taurus energy to thank.

All signs have a propensity to inhabit a Taurus' stark resilience. The relentless determination of an Olympic athlete or the unimaginable drive displayed in city workers hustling for minimum wage, are examples of how the population exhibits the power of this sign. Regardless of how difficult a task is or how long it could potentially take, this Earth sign finds a way to get it done. Even when someone else is awarded an opportunity over them, seeing a job completed righteously is more important than receiving recognition or reward. So, disappointing someone at any cost is a burden a Taurus cannot live with. Coupled with a caring heart that genuinely wants everybody to win, it breaks them when they are perceived to be undependable and/or self-serving. Open your eyes and witness how the planet is littered with dedicated individuals helping underprivileged youth through organizations such as Project Fly LA or local beach cleanup crews committed to keeping the oceans safe for our environment. Taurus energy stands firm on its vow to bring harmony and quality to a system solely focused on monetary gains. If we pay closer attention, everyday people are quietly affirming who they are and mending communities with a strength and resilience that proves beneficial in the end. Taurus energy teaches that going strong and steady builds foundations that are aimed to last for generations. In 1987, as a junior in high school, I struggled with sticking to one thing and applying discipline to my daily routine. I had no idea I would stumble upon the life story of a silent mentor that would teach me the benefits of consistency.

One day, I purchased The Autobiography of Malcom X, by Alex Haley for ten cents at a bookfair, and I fell in love. El-Hajj Malik El-Shabazz, better known as Malcom X, was most notably associated with the Black Muslims out of Harlem, NY, under the guidance of the Honorable Elijah Muhammad. His position with Minister Muhammad was to instill the dignity and civil rights of Black Americans under the guise of Allah and the teachings of Islam. Before he was murdered, he disassociated himself with Elijah Muhammad and the Nation of Islam and founded the Organization of Afro-American Unity (a Pan-Africanist organization). These movements were established to close the gap on racial injustice by including all people of color around the world, in hopes of diffusing and eventually destroying the injustices made on those of African descent.

Malcom was celebrated by many but misunderstood by most. His radical ways were a passionate plea to the world that we must become more proactive in our society, or senseless killings and political corruption will destroy future generations. He was stubborn and quite direct in his approach, during a time when a Black man had no power or authority to speak the truths everyone was witnessing. What I loved most about him was how relentless he was in exposing the truth. He was fiercely dedicated to exposing hypocrites in our government, and traitors in his own movement that neglected to stand on the side of integrity. He was a voice for peace, while examining the resistance to freedom. Even in his steadfastness to remain honorable, he apologized for hurtful and dishonest things he may have said in his pursuit to stand up for a cause that was pulling the entire world apart. Malcom certainly displayed Taurus energy during his thirty-nine years on the planet. Stubbornly fighting for what's right and taking accountability when it was called for. Near the end, he was focused on universal love and harmony in the hearts of all, regardless of the race or nationality you belonged to. I truly believe had he lived longer, his relentless pursuit for truth would have had a larger influence on bringing us all together as one.

Venus is the ruler of Taurus energy, representing all things beautiful and full of love. It harbors a subtle pride that is displayed in everyday life as a universal power forging the desire to celebrate all of God's creations. From the beautiful flowers we spot at our favorite farmers market to the brilliant colors displayed in downtown murals; Venus' intention is to glow with an expectation of admiration. Taurus energy flourishes when the senses are ignited. Beauty is recognized in what we smell, taste, hear, see and feel. Its impact is transformed to the highest form of appreciation when we internalize the aim of respecting our senses to simply, feel good. It's difficult to restrain our joy when a delicious pizza pie makes an entrance in a room or feel a slight tickle when we notice a baby laughing. Taurus energy is responsible for ushering in this important factor of life, sparking the admiration of creation. Beauty and love perpetuate an inner confidence that allows people to express their own beauty, which eventually solidifies ones worth. The Bull is slow and penetrating with its influence like lotion on rough skin. It convinces us all that graceful things can massage hope in our daily lives, even though life may be bleak with challenges and hard times. Surrounding beauty keeps us smiling, in preparation to breathe through another day. Magnifying creation's appeal helps us to begin to see ourselves as the divine beings we were meant to be. Taurus energy implants this goal wherever it goes, so we may eventually and undoubtedly see the beauty within each other; a reflection to be admire.

An early lesson I encountered regarding the importance of beauty and love appeared in an unexpected relationship. Growing up, my mother had a boyfriend who had a daughter, by another woman, a few years younger than me. "Beautiful May" - is how she addressed herself. We loved to share pre-teen boy stories, and any new books we were reading whenever we got together. She was nice, but unlike any other friends I had in Yonkers, NY. My friends were loud and aggressive by nature, with a New York chip on their shoulders. We dressed in Adidas gear with a city swagger that threatened anyone who wished to present a challenge. We were attractive, according to our own standards, and never idolized as "the pretty girls". Being rough, rugged, and raw was our motif. Engulfed in the hip-hop surge we desired to represent. May was quite the opposite. Raised in a suburb of New York City, she seemed far removed from the tough, urban aspects of life. She was tall and modelesque with cocoa brown skin, and long straight black hair that cascaded way passed her shoulder blades. She walked with her chest plate slightly protruding, and a light bounce in her step as she glided across the floor. She strutted with a confidence that could've been perceived many ways. When someone asked her name, she responded, "My name is Beautiful May. Nice to meet you!" Some thought she was a gorgeous, fairytale princess straight out of a Disney movie. Others felt she suffered from conceit that polluted the air and harbored an overabundance of confidence that secretly reminded people of their own shortcomings.

"Conceit" was such a taboo word growing up. We were taught it was ok to be pretty, but always lace it with a sense of humility; never overshadow others or appear to be narcissistic and needy. Girls especially were reminded to stay in their place, respect their elders, and not bring too much attention to themselves. It might have risen from a need to keep us safe from the sick predators of the world, but I believe it may have inadvertently instilled a perception that damaged our self-esteem.

I never thought "Beautiful May" was overbearing with vanity however, full of assurance of who she was. She expressed an obvious outer beauty that I believe originated from an inner stance to inform the world how she wanted to be respected. I admired her positioning. It felt empowering and positive. Is it possible she was being groomed by her family to believe in herself and always expect the best? In retrospect, that's the insignia Taurus energy wishes to leave on the planet, a rooted admiration for your surroundings and all things that make you feel ecstatic to be alive.

Taurus energy is an undisturbed presence that steadfastly makes itself known with an earthbound resolve that cannot be moved or changed without consent. It's reliable and consistent in a world that's constantly reshaping itself and redefining what's important. Taurus people decide what's principal fairly early in life, and rarely do they deviate from their internal plan.

Questions for the Taurus in you:

What areas of your life do you pride yourself on remaining dedicated to?

Where do you feel poverty stricken, and/or a sense of lack? What's the plan to change this outlook?

Are you devoted to promoting your gifts and talents as much as you're dedicated to promoting others?

What beautiful things in your immediate surroundings spark the emotions needed to ignite your creativity?

Haniel's Corner:

Dear Taurus, your energy is indispensable and often times overlooked. You stand rooted to the planet, in hopes to assist in making everything feel loved and valued. Your reliable nature can be taken for granted, as you sometimes present yourself as the martyr for existence. However, remember, you always have a choice to save the world, or not. It's evident you are the soil we continuously rely on to nourish our outdated and complex tasks. You make it all seem so easy to resolve. Remember to take time to reconnect with nature, and let the trees recycle your pain and your silent pleas. You never complain or ask for much but knowing your worth also suggests you keep enough energy for yourself to remain healthy and whole. Thank you for the strong foundation you provide, so that we all feel safe and secure to be our unique selves.

Mantra:

"I bring a guided serenity to the planet when I learn how to consciously move with the flow of the times."

CHAPTER THREE

———— ✺ ————

Gemini - The Master Communicator

"All I need is one life, one try, one breath…
What I stand for speaks for itself…
All I need is one mic…" - Nas

If given the chance, Gemini energy would rule the world with its innate power of the word. As the above quote states, a mic presents an opportunity to express energy through the third constellation of the zodiac. Through a highly charged intellect, and a natural command of language, this air sign can convince you that the world is flat again, sell you ice in Alaska, and wittedly turn the Pope, Baptist. Gemini energy prides itself on bending perspectives and playing devil's advocate, in order to examine different viewpoints. Some may say this tactic is slightly manipulative in nature, however, it always proves to be purposeful. In a world in which we'd like to prove our opinion as gold and better than most, Gemini energy always argues contrasting views to see the "bigger picture" of an issue. We often notice this trait in society within political debates, and lawyers pleading their cases in courthouses; bringing awareness to unpopular topics in order to expose the voice of many, instead of a select few. According to Gemini people, words are an extension of your character. How you describe yourself and/or a situation brings great clarity to how compassionate you are, or how stubborn or unfair you can be. Clear articulation is important when communicating with a Gemini. Always say what you mean and mean what you say. Easy for them, as they possess a rolodex of experiences, quotes, and references in their mind to apply to any subject present. It's quite impressive to watch them jump seamlessly from one conversation to the next, loaded with charm and humor, while schooling folks with unknown facts. Have you ever noticed that one person at a gathering who inserts themselves into a conversation by introducing a completely different topic to discuss, and then quietly leaves the scene? That would be someone with strong Gemini energy, dropping conversational bombs, in order to reveal varied ideas that spawn intellectual growth. Using words to promote a stronger community is a passion that keeps Gemini people motivated.

Consider yourself blessed to have a Gemini as a friend, a colleague, or a partner in crime. Their reverence for words almost always enables them to separate feelings from fact. When seeking their advice or guidance, they consciously decide to remove themselves and their personal opinions in order to fairly assist with reason. Geminis craftily ask qualifying questions to help formulate their outlook, and better serve as a rational confidant. Listening with respect for your journey, and how you've arrived at a point, is paramount; it allows them to give you the benefit of the doubt, based on your reality. Gemini energy seeks solution orientated conversations, rather than an opportunity to place blame. According to them, our choice of words and the right to use them are personal decisions that should be used with responsibility. How we feel about what another says doesn't matter as much as the intention behind the words. I learned this to be true about Gemini energy one day in high school. In the moment, I believed my actions would lead to some obvious emotional reactions, when in actuality, it led to a greater purpose I wasn't privy to yet.

To Mrs. Maher, my 10ᵗʰ grade homeroom teacher while attending Sacred Heart High School in Yonkers, NY, I will be eternally grateful. I believe on some level, she highlighted my voice and gave me wings to fly. Before cell phones and alternate forms of communication, teenagers were forced to pass notes in class that harbored secrets and jokes. In my case, I wrote poems to share with fellow classmates. Some were pieces of art I was proud to create, while others were love notes to my crushes. I began to receive more requests from my classmates to write poems for their girlfriends/boyfriends, only to pass it off as their words. If I had been more entrepreneurial in my youth, I would have charged them a fee for each composition.

One day, Mrs. Maher caught me passing a poem to a friend. My palms began to sweat, my eyes were bigger than saucers, and all I could think was, "My mother is going to kill me!" My mind rushed with so many possible punishments, as my teacher called me to her desk. Saturday detention was for the birds, after school study wouldn't work (I had cheerleading practice) and sitting in the principal's office would be downright humiliating; I'm too cool for that shit. She asked for the paper and read it to herself. To my surprise, she smiled. Not the "this is cute" kind of smile, but a "wow, you're really talented" kind of smile.

"Class, we have a brilliant writer in our midst! She has the choice to read it to the entire class or take Saturday detention for the next two weeks."

I choked on a piece of gum I wasn't supposed to have. I looked at her with confusion, and a semblance of betrayal in my eyes. How could she put my thoughts and opinions and secret wishes on blast? My word was MY word, not hers to unleash. However, I quickly realized what she intended to do, add respect to my literary prowess, maximize its strength, and give the

23

power back to me after recognizing how my writing provoked emotions in others. I would never be the same. So, I chose the former. I read it to the class, and a few stood on their feet in wondrous applause. I was delighted, yet shocked. Even those I hardly spoke to became instant fans of my picturesque thoughts. I noticed this day as the beginning to many occasions I would shine in using the power of the word, Gemini style. Who knew I would be elected to speak to hearts and write words for others that would normally have a difficult time doing so?

Every Friday morning, Mrs. Maher gave me five minutes before the first period bell to express my views to rowdy teenagers, who apparently wanted to hear themselves through my fluid phrases. My creative base felt solid. Through unique formulation of the word, I found my voice. Tearfully, it is a moment in my story I will never forget. I learned that reading poems about teenage love and angst brought a room full of lives together on one accord; all I needed was "one mic". Projecting my truth to stimulate hearts and spark inquisitive minds became a lifelong goal of mine. This is what Gemini energy stands for, the joy and power of reinstating life with selective word choice.

If you are familiar with this sign, you know I can't stop here! Gemini energy is capable of doing more than the average person. This sign has put a new twist on the ancient idea of multitasking. Geminis possess the brain power to effectively reside in seventeen places at once, in order to maximize time and energy spent. They have the makings of the best Hollywood producers that ever lived; managing and compartmentalizing more than two situations simultaneously, in an effort to get the job done. These Twins could walk into a room full of people in obvious disarray, and instantly notice what is causing the problem, adjust their position, and put someone new on a task to create better results. By knowing each person's story, using the right words to encourage performance, and offering needed information along the way, Gemini energy is able to wave its magic wand over any project.

Gemini neatly prioritizes several concerns and/or tasks while executing them without confusion. They rarely get jarred under pressure and remain focused on identifying all the pieces of a puzzle to fit into the whole. It's slightly poetic to watch, like a conductor engineering time. Everywhere we look, we see the artistic flow of Gemini's mental prowess. From the innovative concept of social media to the systematic way a mother of ten runs her household; this is the brilliance of Gemini's binate energy, and how it shows up in the world. The fierce ability to adapt and reconfigure a plan extends beyond being mutable. They are also courageous in risking ideas or concepts that may not work. These Twins thrive on their ability to easily use trial and error, as an unspoken rule, because nothing is a mistake. All possibilities are viable possibilities when they haven't been proven wrong yet. Keeping their options open works in their personal lives, as well. Unlike other zodiac signs, Geminis can juggle five careers, five boyfriends/girlfriends, or five conversations at the dinner table. This gives Gemini energy the freedom to create different identities throughout life that express who they are, completely. Many see the challenge in being considered a "jack of all trades" as being perceived as slightly scattered. However, this sign marvels at the idea of reinvention and possessing many interests. It keeps life intriguing and adventurous. Changing their positions helps them to stay on their toes amidst the twist and turns of their journey. It's interesting to watch people revamp their existence to accommodate a desired direction. Celebrities tend to do this often. Artists often become bored, and rely on

Gemini's ability to switch interests, at the drop of a dime, in an effort to remain inspired.

Some actors can sing and dance, and a few musicians can illustrate and create culinary masterpieces. However, there isn't one artist more captivating and multi-dimensional than Dick Gregory. He began his career as a pioneering satirist who used comedy to ignite thought and encourage debate. His cool approach to humor during his early stand-ups would showcase an extremely laidback individual, often times matter of fact, sitting on a bar stool smoking a cigarette. Mr. Gregory's routines were very reminiscent of an older uncle sitting you down, in a house full of people on a Saturday night, and simply "telling it like it is". Whether he was expressing his opinions on the reason for inflation, or the issue of racism in our country, Mr. Gregory was always prepared to share his truth. An infamous line about a restaurant waitress in the South will always be remembered: "We don't serve colored people here," the waitress said, and Dick responded, "That's alright, I don't eat colored people." Black audiences were his base, however, he crossed over to White audiences as well, charged with the need to intellectually hold White citizens responsible in their role to end the injustices on Black America during the '50s and '60s. Mr. Gregory's instant fame threatened to force him into a corner of comedic royalty, alongside the likes of Redd Foxx and Moms Mabley. However, as the power of multi-dimensional Gemini energy would reflect (even though his Sun Sign was Libra), he began to utilize his platform in multiple ways. His cry against social injustice through his jokes reached a ceiling that garnered little change. So, he went to the streets and fought as a civil activist, bringing attention to himself through the causes he rallied for; the Vietnam War, police brutality, South African apartheid, prison reform, and Native American rights.

In the '80s, he turned his attention on the food industry, after fasting for the aforementioned causes, and developed a nutritional drink mix powder called Slim-Safe Bahamian Diet. In short, he recognized the unspoken slavery, of sorts, food had on the minds of the public, and how we all were being controlled by our diet. If that's not enough, Dick Gregory also became a best-selling author with his novel, "Nigger", breaking down the power of the word and its effect on society. He was on a crusade to highlight many issues artists and politicians were afraid to address. Using several approaches, he vowed to reach as many people as he could. The energy that Gemini conveys doesn't judge your opinions, but rather has a thirst to inform you of issues you may not be privy to. It expands its mental capacity to the likes of Mr. Gregory's, so there's no stone left unturned and no important issue unheard. The vast intellectual capacity of Gemini, the Twins, is mind-boggling and provoking.

Gemini energy is also responsible for being the spark to any social scene, focused on laughter and peripheral, light-hearted fun. This sign has a way of cutting through the mundane, predictable, boring, and routine, in a sheer effort to keep us all fascinated. There are many elements in our society that keep us trapped in our thoughts of despair. The plights of homelessness, elder abuse, and sex-trafficking, just to name a few. One minute, Gemini energy can be knee deep in a debate about any of these issues, and then quickly flip the scene with the best brunch location that brings their peers back to the fun of living again. I'll bet you $20 someone with prominent Gemini energy is responsible for inventing speed dating and baby shower games! The knack for taking a potentially stressful situation and turning it into a memorable experience is genius and done with ease. They pay attention to details that serve as a personal touch. For example: keeping a tally on who will be attending a party they're giving and supplying them with their favorite drink or food item is an important service to them. Unlike Virgos, who are meticulous with the choice of thematic colors and proper silverware, Geminis will make sure an aunt has her favorite alcoholic beverage, the children have a designated place to play, and that seven kinds of cheese will satisfy both the bougie and the "regular folk". They pride themselves on being the "hostess with the mostess", keeping joy as a priority and manageable affection as a guide. Gemini energy urges us to take an extra step in accommodating each other in our daily lives, whether in a public social event or an intimate gathering at home. This sign teaches the world that we all have special needs and opinions, and we should be celebrated for them. As an African American youth, I've witnessed my family and friends display this Gemini attribute quite

effortlessly throughout my life. When you are void of material goods, love is displayed through the power of kindness and an occasional shindig.

My Grandma Jo used to host the most enjoyable Pity Pat parties. Pity Pat is a card game played in most Black communities. It's the arrangement of collecting pairs of suits and/or numbers that add up to enough points to ensure victory. In a small two-bedroom apartment, she would set up several "four-top" tables throughout the living room. The house (my Grandma Jo) would collect a fee from each table as they bet on who would win the game. She often times provided fried chicken, red rice and salad for nourishment. The staple alcoholic beverages - gin, vodka, and rum - would get the patrons loose enough to keep spending their money and play several games a night. As a seven-year-old, I observed playful disagreements that would circulate throughout our dwelling with fascination and sheer delight. I even served as an unofficial (and obviously illegal) bar attendant.

"Sonja, pour half the cup with orange juice and this much," indicated by a finger marker, "with vodka!" I was a master Screwdriver maker! The levity ignited my soul. Everyone knew joy on a first name basis, and lack of money wasn't an issue with copious amounts of love in the room. There were many moments throughout my childhood that resembled this type of celebration. This kept us moving forward, sane, and quite frankly- available to the joy of being alive, despite what we were experiencing as an impoverished family in a low-income area. We survived by recognizing what was important to discuss, and when we were called to release emotions with a great party. This Gemini state of mind is necessary in a world built on competition and fear. We're able to seize the opportunity to relate to one another, void of worry.

Gemini energy is responsible for transmitting what needs to be expressed, in order to alter or define a viewpoint. Regardless of how you interpret it in your life, you must respect it. The ability to make your opinion clear and stand your ground on principal issues, yet be open to and understanding of another's beliefs, is priceless and rare in an aggressive community. I encourage you to pay closer attention as the Master Mind leads you to the broader visions of your surroundings.

Questions for the Gemini in you:

How have you used the power of communication to fuel your purpose?

How can you incorporate the healing medicine of laughter, and the presence of loving souls, to keep you going in times of despair?

Does compartmentalizing confuse you, or empower you to do more with what you have?

When is it necessary to detach your feelings from facts, in order to make informed decisions?

Haniel's Corner:

Dear Gemini, you have a job on the planet that should not be taken lightly. You peruse the globe with an airy disposition that breaks the monotony of relentless ambition and egos that hunger for importance. Please continue to remind us inhabitants that "life is not that deep". Take the edge off of expected lifestyles by showing everyone it's ok to course correct your journey and "keep it moving." Do not let the frustrations of feeling unheard stop you from sharing your expansive thoughts. Most are not privy to the high levels of how you process information. Your intellectual foresight propels you to the next best thing, while others are still figuring out what you did last. Continue to be the change and watch your influence change those around you.

Mantra:

"I use information to clarify any situations that carry dismal thoughts into the light of day. I am the brightest spot in anyone's day, unassumingly leading with my mind."

CHAPTER FOUR

CANCER – The Nourisher

"When I pour into you, life begets life. Oh, but if I stop...
you'll never taste love the same!"

A mother's love is never ending; never fleeting. It snaps into attentiveness in ways other relations fall short. Sustaining admiration for your highest good, your runny nose, your broken heart, your depleted soul. A mother's energy is like an alarm clock to your morning, even if you reside thousands of miles away. It hovers over your bed like a spirit, reminding you that somebody somewhere is rooting for you; always re-introducing you to your "best self" in pleasant, honest and sometimes unpopular ways. Cancer energy represents visceral care and commitment for others, as they utilize all their emotional fortitude to "save your soul". The fourth sign of the zodiac willingly becomes a container for every imbalanced feeling another may experience. This water sign's maternal energy shows up in the world as a soothing touch, a stare of discipline from across the room, or a reassuring smile that makes any rough day better.

Cancer energy provides for, and protects, those they've willingly invited into their hearts. Once the mothering energy of a crab promises to nourish another, they can become quite possessive and will go to any length to keep those they love out of danger. This energy is apparent when a stranger jumps to a child's aid as he/she falls from a tree or someone assists an elderly person across a street with oncoming traffic. We see the love and care of mothering energy constantly, regardless of the gender. It's a magical connection that reminds another that their feelings matter. The Sun Sign of Cancer is always willing to responsibly hold your heart in their hands.

Male or female, Cancer energy shines as a parent who spotlights their offspring as the most important thought, the truest aim, and the deepest devotion ever experienced. Although parenting skills may prove to be imperfect in many ways, this sign is committed to guiding a child's steps with loving nudges of encouragement, and a selfless loyalty comparable to none. This energy is necessary for us all to learn how to soften our approach to the newest members to the world, and carefully groom them into conscious citizens. Some may never get the chance to become parental figures, however, that doesn't mean they haven't had a hand in rearing something meaningful in a child's life. A project, a pet, a collective of students looking for guidance; just a few examples in need of a relentless, caring guardian leading the way.

Humbly, I feel honored to be chosen as a mother of one. This opportunity has been one of the scariest, most demanding, but ultimately the most rewarding undertaking I've ever experienced. I've been calling on the ease of Cancer energy since day one. Motherhood is not for the faint of heart!

On February 28, 2003, I embarked upon a journey that has been shared by billions of mothers. I hung over the staircase banister in our home, almost ten months pregnant, a new mother swollen with life and exhausted by the job I was called to do. At 220lbs, I housed a 10 lb. 1 oz baby while I dilated just 4 centimeters. I dangled my arms in surrender, with parted legs like the solider I was, and howled to a 3 AM moon beyond the walls of our apartment. "This shit is for the birds!" I thought repeatedly. I was sacrificing my sanity for another being plowing through my body; at the moment, it made little to no sense. Imagine an army of unseen entities - your deceased grandma, grandfather, aunts, uncles and a host of others you never met - cheering you on with smiles and fists pumping (Yes, I could see them). The temperature in the room varied; cold one minute, blazing hot the next. The fluctuation in climate confused my reasoning and left me babbling as to why this offering was asked of me. How could I be called to be a mother without knowing what that entails? Who would provide answers to questions that would only be right for this particular individual? Will this same army of ancestral onlookers, deposit money in my bank account if I couldn't find the means to feed both of us? What the heck was I being called to do?!

Kamau was not eager to come just yet, so our planned home birth turned into a hospital visit I wish I could forget. As we awaited a birthing room assignment, our physician, Dr. Goldberg, sauntered in with a hero's smile, convinced he was going to save the day. Upon a quick examination, my water did not break. I was in full on labor, and Kamau stayed lifted high in my belly with no desire to see the world. With the baby miles from the birth canal, I could not attempt to push because it would put us both in jeopardy. So, we made the unpopular decision of having a c-section. I cried. I wailed. I fell into the bed in disbelief. I surrendered to a will I could no longer control. This was not our choice. Soon after, I was wheeled into a room, and the anesthesiologist administered a numbing agent in my spine to seize any pain. As the drugs kicked in, visions flooded my brain of laughing children and tall ancestors, New York pizza and my first boyfriend. By this time, they were rummaging through my body like they were unpacking a suitcase after an enjoyable vacation. Small intestines to the right, pancreas to the left. This shit was STILL for the birds, and without warning; I heard his voice. Kamau gave a high-pitched assurance, prompted by a scream that declared, "Everybody, I am here!" Then, he peed on all three nurses and the doctor! When they placed him on my chest, all of my concerns vanished; I was a mother. All the questions that bombarded my thoughts earlier settled into the convolutions of my brain, primed to formulate answers when it was time to receive them. My ancestors applauded and drifted into thin air. I was a mother looking this greyish brown, perfect baby squarely in the eyes. I became equipped with an energy I'd never experienced. It was quiet and powerful, subtle yet demanding, partnered and cemented. We are in this together, Shorty! I instantly had the courage to be, Mom.

Cancer energy extends its bond as a mother and/or maternal caretaker, while priding itself on curating a peaceful and loving home environment, as well. A Cancer's sanctuary must be sealed with solace and ease. It could be as humble as a studio apartment with one couch and two chairs, but the lingering feeling of loving care makes you want to stay for days. The color scheme stretches from soothing hues of blue and green to toasty orange. Hints of spices, incense, and scented candles own the air, while a choice of music is never remiss in painting the mood. Cancer's world may be intoxicating to those who are rushed to tackle life's responsibilities and leave their abode disheveled. Or, it may be foreign to those who spend less time decorating their home, because they're hardly there. Cancers believe home is an extension of their core, a haven to recalibrate your life's mission in peace and safety. Consider yourself snapped in a Crab's claws if you happen to fall asleep while visiting their nest. Your slumber could very well be a precursor to the capture of your heart.

Cancer also uses food as an offering of nourishment to your spirit. Tasty delights are considered internal hugs this water sign wishes you to consider. They deem sustenance as a way to rebuild and regenerate relationships. Good food is always a remedy to arguments resulting in broken hearts. Need to talk about a challenging situation, how about a little apple pie? Want to celebrate a new promotion, how about sushi?

Cancerians revere food as a door to vulnerable connections. Easing into another's heart cavity so that feelings -good or bad- may be discussed freely, while soothing their woes with flavor and drowning any personal failures with the promise of a full belly. When you're invited to their home to eat, consider yourself highly favored. Regardless of your Sun Sign, I'm sure you inhabit this Cancer characteristic to some extent. Warm biscuits on Sunday morning and smores by the campfire make anyone feel exposed to the loving support the universe desires to give. I had an opportunity to experience this vibration, outside of myself (my Sun Sign is Cancer, by the way). Unexpected and necessary, it took a famous Cancerian to remind me how dope we really are.

About ten years ago, I was invited to attend a party at Forest Whitaker's house. It was a typical southern California summer's day. The weather was perfect for a dip in the pool and drifting lazily with a glass of white wine in hand. I looked forward to relaxing and possibly witnessing some Hollywood shenanigans, more than meeting Forest himself. Honestly, before I knew his Sun Sign was Cancer, I quietly judged him. In my experience, celebrities have proven to be a bit pretentious and often times guarded, in fear of trusting another too much only to be betrayed later publicly. Who knew what he would be like? So, I braced myself and conceded to the thought, "Well, regardless of what happens, at least I can say I visited Forest Whitaker's house." How many people can admit to that?

I pulled into the driveway and smelled the most exotic aromas; food instantly became the super star. Children's' laughter danced through the air, coupled with a sense of home you instantly recognized. Elderly family members were being catered to, and young couples were smooching on lawn chairs; it was a comforting sight anyone could melt into. Shoes off, and a plate full of delicious barbeque in hand, I spotted the guest of honor across the pool. He appeared gentle, proud, and delighted to entertain. Kamau, my then 7-year-old, instantly became his focal point. The two spoke of Legos and soccer, which reminded me of life's simplicity. Hollywood, in that moment, was just a distant dream. Their interaction, and our unspoken understanding of the natural way in which Crabs made everyone family, created an acceptance between strangers that dropped all preconceived notions of his famous status. I relaxed in a strange feeling of belonging, and we began talking about all of the things that made us comfortable; children, food, music, and New York. Too many words can be considered overrated, according to Cancers. Excessive explanation with meaningless words crowds personal space and is void of deeper meanings and emotional connection. As we meticulously sensed our environment, reminiscent of the antennae that leap from a crab's frontal lobe, we quickly accessed the safety of our atmosphere, smiled, and kept it easy. I recognized a shyness in this sensitive artist I dare not challenge with admiring comments of his greatness. Small talk could be quite boring to this cardinal water sign, so we nodded and went our separate ways.

What an honor and comforting surprise to be in the presence of Mr. Forest Whitaker.

Cancer energy is the leader of emotions and intuitive connections. They are able to translate messages from God, ancestors, and Guides with ease, and are always capable of sensing the unseen. It's an innate gift that's misunderstood by most. Have you ever noticed children playfully interacting with the air, claiming they have invisible friends? More than likely, they are communicating with angels on the other side. I'm sure they harbor some form of Cancer energy that enables them to pierce through the veil of spiritual worlds and connect with entities most are not able to see. It's due to their high vibration of emotional intelligence that's often times shunned upon. This sign uses its invisible sensors to seek feelings of love, appreciation, joy, and divinity. The Crab uses its shell to protect a web of sensory nerves that detect the phases of the moon and tides of the ocean. People with Cancer traits are able to do the same, and travel beyond boundaries that society erects, in order to receive instruction from the power source of Spirit, or at the very least, your deeply felt truths.

With a whisper of care and a monsoon of assured strength, once you allow the emotional prowess of a Cancer to invade your heart, you will experience the warmest sensation of inner appreciation. This sign travels love like air waves through your body, with the sincerest eyes and devoted execution to watch you smile again and again. Cancer energy opens up halls of humility and vulnerability you would otherwise be afraid to display. This type of love is patient and relentless in aim, always carrying you with a hint of custody that says, "Your heart is my responsibility, and I will always take on your pain for your highest good." How can we live without the generous devotion of Cancer energy?

With that said, Crabs must be careful how they administer their love. It is a masterful navigation that does not overstep the boundary of the recipient, or themselves. With the same antennas craftily placed atop this crustacean's head that sense the physical environment, they are sometimes signaled to hitch themselves onto the emotional waves of another, without rhyme or reason. Cancers automatically become inundated with problems that have nothing to do with them. Moon children learn to ride the wave and discern which emotions they should become involved with and which should be left alone. I recall a situation like this happening in my own life where I was eager to assist with emotional security, while recognizing the task might be bigger than I could handle.

When I was a teenager, I had a very good friend named Cissy. She was in a relationship with a known drug dealer in the neighborhood who was physically abusing her. To everyone else on the block, he was the nicest guy. He always greeted the ladies with a smile and helped the elderly across the street with their bags as the journeyed home from a long day's work. He dressed nice and smelled better, always sporting the latest gear in the popular colors, and changing his cologne to match the mood. Dude was fly. One day, Cissy came to me with a shocking story of how he'd been beating her at night. At first, I was in a bit of denial. Everyone knew Robin was the savior of the neighborhood, constantly gifting children candy on the weekends and toys during the holidays. The more I listened to her recall the details to the origin of her pain, the more I felt her hurt and knew she was spewing truth. Being the Cancer I am, I internalized her story and made it my own. I became nauseous every time I heard his name. I intuitively knew the exact nights he was beating her, and I began to detect the different inflections in her voice when she feared him most. Her pain became my reality and I decided to do something about it.

I confronted him one night with all the courage in my 5 ft 5-inch, 125 lb. frame. He was on the corner, right in front of the apartment building I lived in. I needed to protect my friend's heart, let him know she had someone that cared for her, and threaten him with lies that my cousins were going to beat his ass if he touched her again. Cissy was across the street when I began to approach him. She saw the glare in my eyes and darted across the road. As I balled my fist with all my might and opened my mouth to recite the words I practiced in the mirror, she stopped me in my tracks, "Sonja, please don't say anything. This is my battle, not yours!" Just like that, I felt a triple blow to my gut. Boom. Boom. Boom. One from him, the other from her, and the last from myself. I overstepped the boundaries of love. My concern for Cissy crossed a personal line, and I was no longer welcome. Now, I had the arduous task of shutting down my care and wiping away the emotional residue that was left. Cissy chose to be harmed and translated love in a way I was unfamiliar with. I could no longer attempt to protect her in ways a Cancer knew how. In fact, I had to put my shell on and stop caring for her the way I did, or else I would suffer more than she did. As a teenager, this was a difficult task. However, for the sake of my health, I had to cut off a sustaining lifeline she could no longer access.

Cancer energy has a responsibility that's not suited for the faint of heart. It's a never-ending projection of emotional concern many are not interested in maintaining. Crabs give love to receive love, protect with love to obtain protection, and nurture with affection in order to be fueled by the same nurturing. It's a revolving door of emotion that rains on all things needing to be fed. It's necessary and often underrated. We all exhibit Cancerian traits, or we would not be available to receive the love we deserve. Learning to sharpen these skills with ease and commitment can foster better relationships on the planet, ultimately respecting the hearts of all.

Questions for the Cancer in you:

How are you willing to nurture in your world?

How do you navigate the scene respectfully, and set up emotional boundaries that lend space for your own emotional support?

What foods, colors, music, or fabric textures influence your feeling of warmth and connection to spirit?

How can you make your home more inviting, in order to invoke a welcoming sense of calm and protection?

Haniel's Corner:

Dear Cancer, you are famously misunderstood by most. Many undermine your sensitivity as a weakness or troubled area in your personality. They couldn't be further from the truth. Your impassioned strength and ancient wisdom add emotional intelligence to a secret fabric that quietly supports the human race. You take care of people's hearts without ever being acknowledged or rewarded. The planet needs you; we will all starve without your genuine care. Accustomed as we are to burying expressions, and shying away from our feelings, you help to explain the healing benefits in making emotions a priority. However, it's necessary to protect yourself from the bombardment of emotions that threaten your health and monitor your rapidly changing moods by taking long baths and visiting natural bodies of water. Remember, the more you love, the more you will receive love. Accepting adverse reactions from a population of people who do not respect feelings will always set you up for disappointment. Continue to believe in your superpower: loving unabashedly from the depths of your soul.

Mantra:

"As long as I feed the world with the genuine goodness of my heart, I will constantly be full!"

CHAPTER FIVE

—◦⁓◦—

LEO – The Generous One

*"Ladies and Gentlemen, coming to the stage, the one,
the only... magnificent Sun!"*

Lights, Camera, Action! Life is one huge performance void of a dress rehearsal. We are summoned to the world stage of our existence with no conscious understanding of how to be human. Everyone is appointed a set of parents, a few friends, a handful of neighbors, several bosses, and then told to handle them the best possible way. Along our journey, responses to important decisions can be emotional or ill-fitting, and can leave us feeling less confident about the choices we've made. Quite frankly, we have no idea what we're doing. Sometimes life calls for our immediate, innate ability to utilize resources for the best possible outcome. Opportunistic, you say? I believe it's a skillful way of thinking and moving on the fly. Regardless what Sun Sign you are, it's a gift we're all equipped with. However, if you feel unsure or inept on how to improv through life, call on the boisterous contribution of Leo, the Lion, to demonstrate.

The ruler of Leo energy is the Sun, a true fire sign. No wonder it roams the planet vibrating as the center of the universe, with high expectations of receiving the same amount of respect, as our galaxy's massive star. Convincing actors, dynamic musicians, and effective executive leaders make up a few occupations of Leo people. When coupled with the joy of creativity and the need to be seen, the Lion wows anyone into submission. Even the quiet types have a glow about them that screams, "You want what I have! You want to be like me, don't you?" A Leo's dynamics often times swallow a room full of people, which can be easily misunderstood. Some read it as overconfidence, overbearing pride, or conceit. Leo's subconscious reasoning behind being the center of attention is to convince everyone how capable we are of living life grandly, and never fading in the shadows of our decisions. The fifth sign of the Zodiac reminds us how important it is to own our steps, show up to win, and always be our "brightest" self.

Performance, or the act of execution, spawns from the need to express. It's pure art to exploit any feeling, message, or passionate belief, and transform it into a palatable experience one can relate to and internalize. The sign of Leo demonstrates the need to inspire, motivate, or support any soulful idea. When a song is sung, or an instrument is played, it originates from the most honest form of communication; the center of Leo's being. This trait exposes their vulnerability and they soon become subjected to judgments of many who are not used to genuine, forthright declarations. However, they are not easily intimidated by the opinions and misunderstandings of another. A Lion's sheer will bypass the slightest criticism, in order to fully express, who they truly are. Have you ever noticed the loudest one at the party with open-ended advice about your love life, or the one with an infectious laugh, handing out compliments, free of charge? You have witnessed Leo energy at its finest. They flutter around a room, charged with life, while urging everyone to join in on their unique joyride of freedom. It can be quite contagious. I recall tapping into Leo energy every time I was poised to hit the stage. A rush of excitement would possess my body, anticipating the exchange of love between the audience and myself. I was prepared to give them everything I got, just like the rays of our magnificent Sun.

Performing with my seven-piece band is one of my life's greatest rewards. As a poet/performer, I bring deep-seated emotions to the written word, and without reservations, boldly place them in a stranger's face. Always accompanied by the "baddest" musicians in Los Angeles, we leave our artistic guts on the stage via the guise of a hip hop/jazz/funk fusion of sound and literary genius. We are always on fire!

One night in late December 1999, I performed at the infamous Temple Bar, located in Santa Monica, CA. It was a modest-sized, live performance venue that held 200 to 250 people. Many great creators frequented this artist hub; Prince, Will.I.Am, and The Roots crew just to name a few. I had gone through a terrible break up with a boyfriend at the time, and my entire musical set was unofficially dedicated to the tumultuous throws of our relationship. I needed to utilize the stage as a conduit of energy to "get over" our experience together. The audience served as a sounding board for those who could relate to our story, while provide support for my healing. Through the generous surge of Leo energy, I extracted truth from my heart and gave that performance everything I had.

Just as our band was called, I remember the trepidation I felt before we hit the stage. I was about to unpack my true feelings like I've never done before. Lies, deception, love, adventures, and personal secrets were all about to be exposed in true form. I had too much integrity to name names, but I knew I had to dispose of this pain in an artistic yet cathartic way. My nervous system got the best of me, and I remember having to take a dump so badly. It was a natural, internal propulsion of my body to release any thing that didn't serve me before I opened my soul and give it all I had. Time did not allow me to use the bathroom. Instead, I paid attention to the spotlight that flashed on the stage, signaling permission to examine every thought, dream, and visceral landscape I was willing to share. That night, I entered from the dark corridors of stage left. Somehow, my heavy breathing and fixated eyes helped to form a protective light around my body as we were about to "go in"! The roar of the crowd began to fade, and a sense of anticipation was felt yet unseen. I looked behind me and sensed the band's eagerness to display a slice of greatness as we were prepared to recall the narratives of our lives, supported by empathic sound. The next six seconds were indicative of a Leo's energetic soft spot; a spiritual, purposeful high we could all learn from. It feels like an out of body experience that lifts you like moisture on the verge of evaporating into the sky. This is the moment you say, "Fuck it!" I travelled to the mic, holding hands with God and praying the nervousness stayed securely in my stomach. I quickly prepared the performer in me to stay in the moment, not harp on any mistakes, and let the feelings fly. I had to speak my peace, and openheartedly was the only way. Upon hitting that first introductory word and sound, the grace of angels began to pour into me. Like light waves of revelations that cannot be seen; like commanding voices reminding you of purpose that no one could ever dissuade you from; like a million butterflies carefully elevating you off the floor. This moment knows, you are sent to reveal unknown creative surges selected for only you to deliver. When Leo energy is ignited within you, as a performer, it is an exhilarating feeling. It's a calling to birth a conversation Spirit hopes to have through you, with any and all that will listen. The crowd jumped to their feet as we opened with an introductory piece called, "When I Step". It laid the foundation for our journey that night. Despite the lessons of love, we all experience, we will forever step with the conviction of a bold and convincing heart. This is the power of Leo, as it relates to performance; be it on stage, in a board room, or teaching a child. When its passion is executed with belief and good intention, truth is easily felt.

A Leo's genuineness never falls short of an opportunity to prove itself. As a lion in the animal kingdom, it is natural to be confronted when you consistently declare to be the most ferocious leader of the pack. A Leo's roar responds with an ego that dares another to give its best shot, and thus possesses the fiercest competitive edge of the entire zodiac. Just stop for a second and look around you. The merciless displays of Leo energy can be found everywhere. From the most ruthless politicians to the loudest and proudest Philadelphia Eagles fans. Defeat is relative, and the contest is never over. It prides itself on the internal fortitude and concentration to see a desired goal to a victorious end. Never shy or yielding, Leo energy will knock you down to get what it wants. This sign's focus is akin to a paralyzed individual determined to walk. Against all odds, Leo always depends on the power of its mind to succeed. Normally, Leo's thirst for contention is with another person. Intently studying their strengths and weaknesses in preparation to sideswipe another's plan and beat them at their game. However, they often take joy in competing with themselves. Applying an extra amount of effort, or a few more hours of study, forces them to remain sharp at their desired sport or craft. Even if a contest has proven to be dangerous in the past, somehow their determination can block out any imminent outcomes. Leo people are motivated by heart, inspired by the impossible, and led by the taste of victory before it arrives at the finish line. It claims the conclusion by seeing it in their mind first; a sure-fire indication that a goal is attainable. Everyone is aware of this dynamic Leo energy. We can use it in our quest to perform better in school, at work, in relationships, or in social interactions. The trick is to never take your eye off the prize, despite outside distractions or cowardice thoughts. A Leo knows it is capable of the unimaginable, because they simply believe they can.

Like millions of people, I was completely captivated by the documentary, "Free Solo". It chronicles the epic feat of rock climber, Alex Honnold, as he attempts to climb El Capitan, a massive, granite rock located in majestic Yosemite National Park. At more than 3,000 feet tall, it is two and a half times as tall as the Empire State Building and more than three times as high as the tip of the Eiffel Tower. The film captures his bold attempt to scale this natural phenomenon, "free solo" (without any harnesses or ropes). With a slight slip of a fingertip, or a misstep of his left foot, he is primed to fail. El Capitan is almost completely vertical, and nearly void of any deep crevice to aid Alex in the climb; making this the most frightening undertaking anyone has ever witnessed. The film displays Alex's sheer will and determination to defeat the enormity of this rock. Using the mental prowess displayed by Leo the Lion, he tapped in and succeeded. Despite a few emotional outbursts, concerns of his then girlfriend, and a bad fall he experienced during a practice run that resulted in a broken ankle, he continued on the conquest. After healing from his fall, he strategically scaled the rock in a harness, while mapping out the proper routes to execute his dream. Alex then acquired a needed tunnel vision that seemed to block out the film crew and drones that recorded his climb. He was completely "locked in" and determined to push himself past his limits. Alex's competitive edge surpassed what most people would encounter and left his spectators with a taste of how Leo energy wishes to defeat and conquer. This sign is on a mission to discover opportunities that toy with the most difficult comfort zones one could establish. Surprisingly, sometimes in the most lighthearted, joyous way.

Laughter and fun-loving events bring the best out of Leo the Lion. They marvel in the delight of new adventures, filled with wonder and innocence. You've never met a Leo that doesn't have a strong affinity for children. Partly because they consider themselves "one big kid", they're always discovering new and creative ways to approach life; akin to lazily building sandcastles by the shore and watching them wistfully wash away in the minutes that follow. Nothing should be taken too seriously, and life is created by the trust they have in themselves and the expected celebration that follows. This sign highlights the childlike delight of the simple things, and the joy it brings anyone bearing witness.

Leo energy takes pride in protecting the innocence of children, as well. Recognizing the need to step in, when necessary, and speak on their behalf. They identify with the importance of preserving their right to be free and untainted before they are launched into the throws of adulthood. This sign finds satisfaction in teaching children about the pitfalls and many options that can be presented in life, while relentlessly encouraging them to reach beyond their expectations. Leo energy believes that through the eyes of children we all have permission to dream and ignite our passion in ways we've never imagined. Pouring into children, and giving them the attention needed to grow, excites their curiosity and makes them better informed grownups. I've noticed certain government leaders have refused to recognize our younger generation as a priority. They continue to short-change their educational institutions and art/music programs that are proven to aid in their success. Through my experiences with mentoring teenagers throughout Los Angeles, I can attest that city officials would greatly benefit by taking a page out of a Leo's book. Investing in the joy of our children will surely make the world a more fortified, enjoyable place to live.

While pursuing my artistic career in my early twenties, I was forced to take random jobs to support myself. One in particular not only helped pay my bills, but virtually changed my life. A good friend alerted me about a job opportunity assisting children who were wards of the state. These were children who were taken into custody by Los Angeles County, due to their parents abandoning them, or deemed unfit due to consuming controlled substances or incarceration. My position was to watch over a group of twelve boys between the ages of ten and fifteen years old. I worked in the house for eight hours a day cleaning, cooking, providing medications, enforcing schoolwork, and taking them on needed outings to the mall or the beach. They were from diverse backgrounds and stories, which made it incredibly difficult to relate to them at first. There wasn't one way to approach them all. Compassion was required to learn what inspired them, in order to assist them in overcoming their circumstances. On one hand, this was the most enjoyable job of my life. As a single woman at the time, with no children of my own, I enjoyed the few outings to the roller-skating rink, or having water balloon fights in the yard of the house they lived in. Being with them awakened a sense of wonder and exploration I hadn't felt in years, which took me away from the seriousness of adulthood and the pressures of paying bills on time. These boys unexpectedly added a delight to my world I wish I could repay them for.

Simultaneously, I felt I was in a position to take care of them, nurture them, and guide them in certain areas of their lives where they may have lacked or needed some redirection. This area of the job always proved to be a little tricky to navigate. You're never supposed to lend your heart in positions like these. Allowing your feelings to consume you about a young adult, when you don't have legal rights to take care of them, can set you up for disappointment. I could not shake the Leo disposition instilled in me, even if the state of California only paid me to follow certain procedures to keep them healthy until they were eighteen years old. I tried to fight for their rights in areas that left me exhausted; better food choices, fewer medications that shut down their emotional responses and left them lethargic throughout the day, and enabling communication between certain parents and their children, because they periodically showed a real interest to connect with family (this always put a smile on the boys faces). I was a rebel within a system that could care less about their overall welfare and was more concerned about the money these facilities were receiving from the state government to take care of them. The magic of Leo energy was certainly used while employed there. Always fighting to maintain their innocence and wonder in growing up, until they were forced into the harsh world of responsibility. I always wish I could've done more. After two years of working for the state, I realized my voice was falling on deaf ears. The muscle and tenacity of one, twenty-something year old from New York, was unable to change a system that had been in place for decades. I pray that my compassion for them lingered in their later years, prompting them to make the best decisions necessary for their lives.

Leo the Lion remains indicative of the Sun's energy, which infuses souls with pride and encouraging words to remain courageous in the face of inevitable change and challenge. This sign leads with heart and pure desire. Always exhibiting the type of will that fosters results; a will that creates opportunity for all. We are blessed to experience such a generous declaration to the planet that prompts us to live fully and unabashedly.

Questions to ask the Leo in you:

How courageous are you in visiting areas of your life that you've silenced, due to fear?

Where do you need to play more, and relinquish the need to be serious?

Do you hold high expectations in life, and how often does it lead to disappointments?

When was the last time you allowed someone to love you with the same amount of passion you love them?

Haniel's Corner:

Dear Leo, you are the gift that keeps giving, and the provider that never asks for love in return. Even though you want to see everyone win, please be aware of this impossibility. Some will not shine in the ways you deem necessary, and others do not have the desire. It can sometimes be a little daunting to push your agenda on those that would rather live ordinary lives, in an ordinary way. Your best plan to encourage those around you is to shine, whether they are watching or not, and meet them where they are in life. Be the sun and watch the inhabitants around you grow in the process, just because.

Mantra:

"I give and receive from my heart to remind us all to begin and end everything in life, with the miracle of love."

CHAPTER SIX

VIRGO – The Caretaker

"Service is a noble act most narcissists cannot spell.
They have Virgos and Alexa for that."

Virgo the Virgin orchestrates life with subtle grace and masterful precision. They pride themselves on being unnoticed, but they're absolutely aware of the importance they carry throughout the world. Known for being "Johnny on the Spot", this earth sign tidies the planet in ways many take for granted. It's difficult to recall a problem when a Virgo is present. They instantly pounce with a solution before anyone can utter a word. I often say that if we didn't have the presence of Virgo energy, our existence would be in constant disarray. Many more homeless people would go unfed, elderly people would

be forgotten about, and most nurses would lack the tender care needed to assist the ill. This sixth sign of the Zodiac selflessly offers its expertise, time, care, and love to make another smile and feel fulfilled. Virgo energy is subtle in its approach and gentle in its delivery, yet always steadfast in its purpose to get a job done. They work tirelessly to complete a task by exhausting every resourceful option in order to assure satisfaction. If a Virgo elects themselves to help you, consider yourself vetted before they issue assistance through inquisitive questioning and acquisition of your character.

According to them, it's imperative to know how to aid another without wasting time or effort. This sign acts as a humble servant to humanity that looks for nothing in return; willingly stomping out brush fires before they extend into potential catastrophes. We can all partake in the considerate energy of Virgo, in an effort to make this world a better place. Simply find a way to assist, knowing that smiles and appreciation are the goal, not ego and gain. I had a glimpse of this sign's nobility growing up. Pegged as a child who made it a habit to bring home stray animals for my mother and I to care for, if others didn't have the wherewithal to help the needy; why not me?

City Park Projects in New Rochelle, NY was my early childhood stomping ground. A brick building complex occupied primarily by Black people in the early 70's. Honestly, it was one of the highlights of my life. There's an incredible stigma placed on low income living. Often times, it's compared to what the well-to-do deem important in this society: "Go to school, go to college, have a family, get rich, and then die." Well, according to universal and spiritual law, we are all not equipped for that journey; neither do we care to have it. So, many from the outside see project life as dismal and destructive. However, I remember an abundant amount of love issued in a plethora of ways.

Celeste was a hardworking single mother who counted every penny. Life was a budget. Time, energy, money, clothes, joy, bullshit, and food were all accounted for. Engaging in too much or too little of any of those things, created problems and lack. As a child, no one tells you the severity of giving away what you have. If you notice it, it's there for all to share, right? Well, one day, I found out the hard way.

After school, my friends and I were hungry. They must've served something extremely unappetizing that day at Bernard Elementary School, because we all busted through my front door famished. Allowing myself in, as the proud latch key kid I was raised to be, we helped ourselves to something to eat. Peanut butter and jelly wouldn't do, tuna fish was boring, and there wasn't enough bologna meat to fry for everyone. However, there was a juicy steak staring at us all from the lower shelf of the refrigerator. Red and mouthwatering, we opened our eyes wide to initiate the pursuit. I paused for a quick second, "My mother wouldn't mind if we helped ourselves to the steak, would she? I'm being of service. My friends' parents might not need to prepare dinner for them later, because they already ate at our house." Aiding in the spirit of sharing, I commenced to preparing the untouchable, juicy steak. We enjoyed every bite; laughing in contentment, and grateful for such a filling meal. A few hours later, my mother entered our apartment already aware something was done without her permission. The air smelled of spices and meat. My friends quickly gathered their belongings, in anticipation of a storm, while I stood in the kitchen with the most innocent grin across my face. Before she could ask what happened, I quietly stated, "I just wanted to help, Mommy." After finding out what occurred, she was furious that we ate the "good food" being saved for a special occasion, but she was also proud I had the heart to risk an act of kindness despite what she might have thought. My friends' happiness in that moment was worth the repercussions. This act of kindness was so indicative of Virgo energy; always prompted to share.

Our society keeps us conscious of what we should contribute, and what we should not. A homeless person can receive your leftovers, but do you think twice before buying them an actual meal? Companies manufacture more products that exhibit less quality, in order to produce more, which makes them more money. On the onset, it's deemed more practical by nature, but garners less respect for the consumer. Virgo energy is pure and rarely recognizes money over need. It's a gift, within the naivete of a Virgin, is to serve your heart while simultaneously paying attention to details. You see this sign's energy on a daily basis when we check our "to-do" list, secure vital information, or notice a piece of lint on a friend's new outfit. Virgos are born to dissect what's presented to them, almost like cracking binary codes with the purpose of revealing top secrets. They take pride in any process, believing they play a significant role in building the whole. In the mind of this earth sign, details reveal order, and order potentially leads to perfection. You begin to appreciate the magic of this energy when it's displayed in the art we have grown to love. Look at the work of some of your favorite celebrities. Their display of accuracy defines the amount of care and integrity this signs energy wishes to convey. Regardless of your personal opinion surrounding the following celebrity, no one can discredit the amount of diligence he displayed throughout his life; straight Virgo vibrations.

Michael Jackson was a supernova! He was an entertainment phenom that rocked the planet with an insurmountable gift the world may never see again. Besides the fact he came from a talented family, fans would consider him a musical genius' for his meticulous Virgo ways displayed within the details of creating music. Even though he didn't formally play an instrument, he consciously knew the role of each part featured in his music. During producing sessions, he would hear the strings or the piano in his head, and carefully execute it to hired musicians to play. Note for note, and chorus to outro, he could dismantle a song like arbitrary raindrops creating a composition as they fell from the sky, only to arrange them into monster hits that appealed to billions of people. Virgo precision, at its finest! I viewed a documentary once that showed him exhibiting the art of beatboxing before hip hop cemented its place in history. Using rhythmic cadence, with the help of his mouth, lips, throat, and tongue, he would intricately breakdown the sections of a drum kit. He syncopated up to seven different sounds, while simultaneously creating dynamics and accents with his hands and feet. Every second mattered and every note of the drum was accounted for. It has been said of the "Off the Wall" album that he completed over one hundred songs and chose twelve to fifteen of them for the project. His level of detail and precision was overlooked by the masses, because we became so enthralled with the persona rather than the talent. However, I would argue his level of practical accuracy separated him from the pack. There was no such thing as being frivolous and throwing caution to the wind. Every feeling was accounted for, and every note had meaning.

His appreciation for detail was also apparent in his live shows. Although many successful artists are known for elaborate stage shows that amaze stadiums full of people, none dazzled like Michael Jackson's. He was a tireless worker who prided himself on the exactness of things. If he wanted to promote fantasy, his audience would receive every nuance of that vision. If he wanted to exhibit different cultural influences in his show, he did so with integrity and respect. Many dancers and stagehands were interviewed, admitting they were challenged in keeping up with his energy level and how amazed they were by the level of thoughtful innovation within his shows. Explosions, several dozen dance sequences, an army of musicians, and costumes were all orchestrated by the master mind of this hardworking Virgo. Imagine if we all had half of the dedication and focus of his selfless energy. We would feel more accomplished and satisfied that our purpose actually contributed something precious and distinctive to the community. In essence, that is the goal of Virgo the Virgin, giving the world and its inhabitants everything needed to thrive to ultimate excellence.

Virgo energy doesn't set out to achieve hero status, however. Honestly, they don't believe in an image so finite. They are on a continuous quest for perfection that requires them to be in constant review of themselves, and the world around them. Virgo energy thinks of a goal, prepares for it, and gathers the necessary tools for executing the plan. I often equate them to a glorified stage manager, sticking to the blueprint of any production and making sure everything is held together with a carefully selected cast and crew that's well-informed of their responsibilities. Overseeing every moving part to ensure that they perform their duty for the enjoyment of the whole. Virgo energy works as a sacrificial component to every task it performs, in order to deliver exactly what it promises. The world holds many examples of this energy; from the execution of an intricate surgery to the exact precision of a glass blower; from the accuracy of a scientist to the mathematic intricacies of an astronaut. These occupations go above and beyond the task at hand, refining information every step of the way. The challenge with securing "perfection" is that it doesn't exist. We all live in an imperfect state of perfection. Universally speaking, everything is happening exactly as it should. So, although it's admirable to strive to such unearthly heights, Virgo energy must constantly remind itself to do its best and let the powers that be do the rest. I learned this valuable lesson in my youth, looking for ways to overcompensate my skills, in an effort to show I could perfectly and successfully be of service. Virgo energy must remember that their "little bit" is a lot better than anyone else's maximum effort.

Attending Bernard Elementary School was a milestone moment in my life. Receiving a liberal, early education from a multiracial staff of teachers, in a massive three-story stone building. It was reminiscent of a castle built during the turn of the century, sturdy and able to last another two hundred years. We walked from City Park Projects to school, through wooded terrain, via a path paved out over the years by little feet eager to learn. All of the children in the neighborhood attended this school. We journeyed there together, we fought, we stole each other's girlfriends and boyfriends, and we created together. Before budget cuts on art and music were a concern, the '70s provided a plethora of programs to showcase talent, to keep the youth busy, and to spark imaginations. One day, my music class was asked to create wooden drums. Small, rectangular, twenty-inch long, five inches wide, and three-inch-deep drums to paint and glaze and be made anew. After designing our specified instruments, we were judged on our creations to win a prize. My friend Nicole was apprehensive about designing hers, so she asked me to do it for her. Being the "good friend" I hoped to be, I complied. I created a picturesque beach scene where the shoreline met the ocean, and a few seagulls enjoyed their flight over two beach goers soaking up a clear, sunny day. That was it. Nicole was so happy with what I created, it made me proud. However, mine was going to be better; it was a competition, after all. The urgency of perfectionism kicked in, and I overcompensated in areas her drum did not display. I created the same scene as hers but added more detail to seek excellence. Smiling bike riders on a path down the shore were included, as well as a man playing catch with his dog in the middle of the sand and three sailboats, all of different shapes and sizes careening on the ocean blue. I was sure to win. In my mind, the particulars were noticeable, and I clearly cared more about my drum than what Nicole's drum displayed. As the teacher made her rounds, absorbing the great creations of budding, future artists, she made her decision: Nicole's drum won! My friend and I both looked at each other in amazement. Without revealing to the teacher who the real creator was (obviously, we would get in trouble for cheating), Nicole hugged me in delight, whispered, "Thank You," in my ear, and proceeded to march up front to receive her gift. I sunk in my chair, not knowing what to make of my loss. Then, it hit me! Even at a young age, I knew I did "too much". I searched beyond artistic integrity to capture magnificence, with the burden of being perfect. It backfired on me, and two lessons were learned. Number one, do your own work! And two, perfection is a myth created in the minds of those who are afraid to take chances of creating what's felt, and not what's expected. I'm grateful to have acknowledged this lesson early on in life.

Virgo energy is something we all can call upon in the world. There's always someone to assist, and some cause to lend our expertise to. This sign asks that we all wake up to the call and recognize that we are in constant need of each other. It would benefit us as a human family to pay more attention to the details that often go unnoticed. You never know, we may collectively end a catastrophe before it has a chance to begin.

Questions for the Virgo in you:

Do you have one person to call on when you are in dire need of practical assistance?

Have you ever felt the need to exhibit perfection, just short of insanity?

Do you confuse the need to rationalize with the delusion of denial?

What day have you scheduled on your calendar as a "me" day?

Haniel's Corner:

Dear Virgo, thank you for your sweet altruistic ways. You keep the planet moving forward with care and organization that many are ill-equipped in presenting. Be aware of how much time and energy you are outsourcing and save a little for yourself. We need you healthy and whole to do the jobs others will not. Forgive yourself more for making mistakes you may have had no control over. Your need for perfection is appreciated, however, we all know you are human. Continue to grow by allowing change and flexibility into your sometimes rigid, approach to life. If you haven't heard it lately, our lives are better because of you.

Mantra:

"Perfection is an illusion. Everything I do is right and exact, in the light of God."

CHAPTER SEVEN

LIBRA - The Enchanter

"I'll invade the contours of your mind, dizzy them with charm, and force you to become my partner in crime - I'm that good!"

Libra energy appears like a vision you once imagined, a dream you once experienced, and certainly a soft, manipulative presence capturing you with charisma and varied knowledge that could stretch a conversation for days. This sign investigates your mental capacity, assesses your intellectual property, and relates to you according to their findings. Have you ever experienced a detective at work, or watched a great newscaster ask probing questions? Consider yourself snatched by the magnetism of the seventh sign called Libra energy. This leader of the mind dissects motives in the midst of a conversation, with class and ease focused on facts and highlighting what's just. According to Libra energy, most people are predictable and sadly unoriginal. Within minutes of talking with someone, Libras already knows how the story ends. Based on the information and the players, they think to themselves, "I've seen this scene before," and take pride in knowing the ending before it arrives. This dispels the notion of them being duped. Libra's dislike being fooled or taken advantage of, so they must quickly figure a story out in order to mentally prepare them for what could follow. Libra is an air sign mastermind, and exceptional at demanding what it wants from people with an undeniable desirability. Akin to a princess or a prince commanding their court, Libra cleverly influences your thoughts to assure you that what it wants, is an idea you've already had. They pride themselves on weighing out the pros and cons, and skillfully utilizing information to obtain what's best for everyone involved. Libra energy finds the most creative solutions to problems everyone may be fretting over. They lead with a realistic and fair approach, exhaust every possible outcome before opening their mouths. This gift can be acquired by any sign, if we're willing to learn, keep cool under pressure while innately knowing there's a resolution lurking in the midst of programs, resources, or a wise elderly person who may potentially save us all from panic and destruction. Consider adopting some of Libra's inherited intellectual prowess; it may get you out of some of the darkest times of your life.

My mother is the consummate Libra. A magician at managing circumstances, who finds every possible way out of any dilemma with precise thinking. She is my shero, imperfect in ways, yet never succumbing to failure without giving a well-thought-out, earnest fight. One Christmas, when I was ten years old, my mom seemed void of joy. Financial difficulties soon revealed themselves to be the source of her unusual silence.

"We may not have a tree this year, Sonja," she said, almost haphazardly. "Not sure how good of a Christmas we will have."

I was too excited to care. Visiting family, eating plenty of food, listening to the Temptations' Christmas album, and opening presents was a stellar celebration in my eyes.

"It doesn't matter, Mommy. We got each other!" I responded.

I meant it with every morsel of love I possessed in my young, yet mature mind.

I tried making her laugh by cracking corny jokes I'd learned from some neighborhood children and campaigned for smiles by talking mess about how my great grandmother would lick her fingers when she cooked; anything to shake her out of the pensive mood she harbored. I just knew whatever we were faced with, she would make it alright.

Apparently, that realization wasn't enough for her. She sat quietly for a few minutes, determined to make things better for our small family unit. Suddenly, like a light turned on in her mind, she was lovingly bossing me around with ideas to restore Christmas and renew her spirit.

"This is what we're going to do. Here's $20. I want you to walk down to the end of the street, to the Christmas tree lot, and find whatever tree you can get with this amount of money. Tell Charlie, the guy that works there, you are my daughter. He'll help you out; I think he likes me," she said with a smile. "I'm going to stay home, make us a good dinner, and begin stringing some lights, so it looks a little festive in the house. Call your friend, Sue, and ask her if she wants to spend the night. You girls can stay up as long as you like. I promise, we'll make the best out of what we have."

I believed her and set out on my mission. It was snowing in New Rochelle, NY that day. About 6 inches fell in freezing temperatures, which made my trek gleefully arduous; a ten-year old walking through blistering winds, planning to do my part. Charlie was closing the gate as I approached, and I began to scream.

"Charlie! I want to get a tree for me and my mom."

He quickly shoved me to the side. "Sorry, baby. It's two days before Christmas. I have to shop with my wife and get out of this cold."

"Please, mister. I only have $20, but my mother said you would help me." I begged shamelessly at the gate with the cutest face I could muster.

"Who's your mother?" he asked in a New York, bossy type of way.

"Celeste!" I shouted back.

"Celeste is your mother? Oh, come right in. She's a good woman, and always helps with my mother's health issues, being a nurse and all. I adore her. Come on in!"

Delighted by his kindness, and even more appreciative of my mom being a good person who people would do favors for, I walked in. There weren't too many choices left, being so close to the big day. I had no idea what to choose.

"Do you have anyone to help you?" Charlie asked.

"No, just me!"

"How much money do you have?" he asked.

"Just $20."

He chuckled lightly, in playful disbelief.

"Here's what you do. Take this small tree that only has leaves on one side for $20. It'll be easy for you to drag through the snow. When you get home, put the side with no leaves against the wall, so no one can see it. Ok? No one will ever know."

I smiled the biggest smile, and simultaneously dreaded walking back home through that snow, but we had a tree and Christmas was alive and well again.

"Thank you so much, Charlie! You're a nice man." I handed him the money and began my journey through the soft terrain. Excited to decorate our runt of a tree, but mainly to see a smile on my mom's face. The lesson I learned that day came from Charlie and my mom (he must've been a Libra, too): regardless of what you're going through, and whatever circumstances impede your steps, think hard enough of a plan that can change your reality. There are many solutions and great people on the planet, as long as we are willing to assist each other in finding the way.

Libra energy knows no one can truly succeed without integrity, honesty, and genuine connections with good people. This sign displays a commitment to fairness, so we can all experience justice and create win/win situations. Libras pride themselves on the nobility they possess to do the right thing. According to Libra energy, balance and restoration in any life situation is imperative and necessary. Those who harbor the energy of this sign can be found in the center of most disagreements or healthy debates, explaining alternative viewpoints in an effort to view every angle to a story. What's the point of sharing information, if we can't openly express varying perspectives? Libra energy promotes order that invites clarity, appoints responsibility, and devises a plan to ensure everyone's needs are met. If not, they believe in consequences. With a keen sense of reading someone's character and their story, they have a knack for recognizing deception. Libra energy believes if you delude others, then you have gone to ridiculous extents to be someone other than who you are and, therefore, cannot be trusted in their eyes. Whatever aspect of life you're associated with becomes minimized. The Libra becomes the judge, the jury, the lawyer, and even the court guard when you have beguiled them. Assessing your story, giving the verdict, and looking for reasons why you committed the crime in the first place, is their process. Soon after, you are thrown in their proverbial jail, and you will never get a second chance to be an integral part of their life. If you are defined as an unjust person, you will forever be seen as such, and you can't argue their decision. Like the greatest politicians alive, Libras know where you stand, they don't hold grudges and, ironically, are able to still sit at the table and dine with you the next day. They know who you are, and how far they can go with you. Libra's teach us the wisdom in accepting people as they are. They are akin to your toughest coach. You may harbor ill feelings for them pushing you to uncomfortable heights, but you respect their position and you know their actions may eventually teach you something. The art of equanimity is to never take it personal, just be able to intellectually assess your surroundings with truth and detachment, and then move on. We can all be inspired by some of the greatest who ever inhabited this trait. A dynamic disposition that navigates a myriad of personalities would describe one of the greatest peacemakers that ever walked the planet.

Rev. Dr. Martin Luther King Jr. was a sun sign Capricorn, but definitely adapted to the art of justice harbored by Libra energy. He was one of the greatest men in history who stared injustice in the eyes and dared it to state a ridiculous claim. He fought hatred with love, evil with song, and sickening traditions with the intention of God. He demanded those who chose a limiting life of racism and pain to own up to their crimes, and change. Plain and simple, Dr. Martin Luther King Jr. considered law a doctrine of truth, and that we all should hold ourselves accountable. When presented with facts of bloodshed and broken families, systematic ploys, and obvious tyranny, he had the ability to accuse the guilty, forgive them, and build together. Using his charm and fun-loving wit, Dr. King assisted in magnetizing the masses and courageously convincing the oppressors that he was the man with the master plan; appearing mostly unphased and convinced that life cannot be swayed in the imbalance of humanity, but rather secure itself in the decency of togetherness. He embodied the vital Libra energy of pooling resources and information that would be sensible enough for a young child to understand and convert any unfair thoughts into viable solutions. He encouraged individualism, but not at the expense of harming another. Civil unrest in the '40s, '50s, and '60s was as plain as the nose on our faces, and he propelled forthright human beings to abolish it. A thoughtful leader, and an architect of time, he proved togetherness was the only way of the future. Dr. King lived his life focused on teaching us the power of sharing space and respecting the sanctity of another. In this way, he inhabited another memorable trait of Libra energy.

Partnership, of any kind, is a vital component of the Libra Sun Sign. They have the propensity of discovering varying opinions and insights of others in order to reach a common ground. They make some of the best husbands and wives, business partners, and colleagues, with the idea that relying on another's better half solidifies a better whole. Libra energy always considers another's plight, shortcomings, and gifts, as long as they are honest and integral in their intentions. In any relationship, they are like the recordkeeper of successes, failures, losses, and triumphs, in order to keep account of how their partner is growing. These tally marks may come off as petty to some, but securing the facts keeps the bond fair. They have a way of picking up the slack in order to support the shortcomings of their partnership. Much like any dynamic duo - Batman and Robin, Thelma and Louise - they are always on the mark; assisting with a word of encouragement, a joke to relieve any stress, or running errands for you while you take a well-deserved nap. However, Libras must always remember themselves in the equation. Often, if they are busy highlighting a mate, they slide into the identity of the other and lose the essence of who they are. Keeping their own interests and hobbies are vital for them to show up as a whole person who's secure enough to handle themselves and their mate.

I learned the essential lessons of partnership in an unlikely situation, being an integral member of my high school cheerleading squad. Before I emerged on an organized team, such as the Sacred Heart High School Cheer Squad, cheering was a mere hobby with the neighborhood children. A lot of our childhood cheers were musical in nature, reminiscent of dance steps that didn't require much athleticism. It was pure, unadulterated fun. We gathered once a week to practice and go over new cheers to present for our Sunday games. Our parents watched as the young boys played football, keeping score and marveling at fantastic plays. Our cheerleading duties were somewhat loose. We were focused on being cute with easy-going duties. The coach of our team was a teenager, and the requirements of our captain concentrated less on responsibility and more on bragging rights.

However, in high school, cheerleading became a major focus. It was a sport that called for tumbling skills, flexibility, and most of all, partnership. The team was accountable for one another as we implemented staggered positions, intricate routines, and choreography that included isolated, rippling movements that suggested mastered precision. However, partnership between the captain and myself required a sense of balance I never imagined.

I was appointed co-captain early on, an honor that was not readily given to an incoming freshman. Normally, you need a year before you can prove yourself worthy. I was awarded the challenge based on my prior cheer-leading history and knowledge. This was the first time I had to share ideas and information effectively. Initially, it was natural for me to express what I wanted and expect people to comply. In my earlier years, that's how you were taught; just go along with what's offered. I figured it worked like that always. I quickly learned there's an art to becoming a leader in a position that partners with another great mind. You cannot bully a contributor into seeing your vision over another's. Compromise, compassion, and complete surrender are attributes to great partnering. Often, putting yourself in your teammate's shoes, and asking proper questions, leads another to necessary conclusions. You are then able to speak to their needs and fears in a way that assures your fellow teammates are considered and appreciated. Even teenage girls on a high school cheerleading squad have opinions and egos, sensitivities and boundaries, fears, and common denominators. It was the first time I realized that my way was not the only way. My captain had par-ticular cheers and work ethics I needed to respect, in order to maintain a decent camaraderie within our squad and deliver the best performance for each game or competition. This push and pull, give and take, wasn't easy but it was necessary. It highlighted a long journey we all share. As we seek harmony on the planet, we must learn to coexist as earthly companions.

Libra energy has a responsibility to inject happiness into the world via the art of fellowship. This sign has been given the innate ability to bring people together with ease, while highlighting each other's gifts and celebrating our truths. It's amazing to watch the orchestrating energy of this sign lead the brilliant thoughts of others with hope and fairness.

Questions for the Libra in you:

What hobbies or self-interests do you engage in that secure your identity, while in a relationship?

Do you construct long lists of pros and cons that leave you stifled in indecision?

How often do you find the median in a situation to ensure that everyone wins?

Do you overthink a scenario, based on what you believe is true, only to create false allegations against someone or something?

Haniel's Corner:

Dear Libra, people feel safe sharing their ideas and discoveries with you. They know you'll ask intriguing questions that help them build upon their success, while keeping everyone in mind. Your energy carries throughout social circles, because you are needed to bring a multitude of personalities on one accord. You quickly assess situations under pressure, and mediate disputes that could potentially linger in time. Your energy must hold the smallest crook accountable before it festers into generations that have the potential to destroy themselves. Charming Libra, never take your gifts for granted, and apply that same strength and resilience you give to others onto yourself. Making decisions to take risks and forge forward in life, can only be successful if you practice and go for it. What are you afraid of? If you make a decision to jump into something, and it doesn't work, there will be more than enough people and opportunities to support your comeback.

Take a little for yourself and leave the defense of cynicism at the door. Walk with confidence knowing that most people want all people to win!

Mantra:

"I trust the support I issue to another will easily and effortlessly find its way back to me!"

CHAPTER EIGHT

SCORPIO – The Observer

"If I capture you, will you resist?
...Take you beneath a mound of superficial entanglement.
...Whispering my demands, carried like confetti mist across my lips.
Would you be mine, and prepare for the most passionate ride of your life?"

Scorpio energy pushes boundaries, in order to discover comfort in the unknown. It seeks experiences against the norm, and unearths extraordinary, forbidden mysteries of life. There's an innate audacity the Scorpion carries, while using curiosity to prove there's power and importance in the unseen. They wish to discover answers that mere humans cannot provide. Whether it's received through deep-seated thoughts, the mystical spirit world, or buried information spanning centuries, this eighth sign wishes to explore uncharted territory to reveal the superficiality of the surface mind. Scorpios believe in hidden treasures that explain the conversations of the universe, medical miracles that cure baffling diseases, and love so untainted it could change the world. They put forth effort to recognize abilities so deep, you may find it impossible to discover it within yourself. When Scorpios look at you, they travel past your eyes and dive deep into your soul to learn your true intentions for being present in their lives. Deep and focused gazes determine how worthy you are to receive the commitment of a relationship with them as well as gauging how much attention to a project they should be committed to. This hyper-sensitive water sign does nothing superficially. They give one hundred percent of themselves when they see an opportunity to grow or help another achieve a goal. Other sun signs would rather debate about the state of global affairs, in an effort to show their intellectual prowess. However, Scorpios deem emotional intelligence paramount, and sense what's good for them rather than assess logically. Have you ever had a friend to elect himself or herself as the unofficial cop on a night out with rowdy friends? Watching the scene and quietly keeping everyone safe? Or maybe you've planned a family gathering only to have a spouse quietly awake hours earlier to scope the party area for items dangerous to toddlers lurking in the midst? These are sure examples of a Scorpios keen yet emotional foresight. Rather than talk about what needs to be done, they jump to action of their heightened emotional awareness, and explain later.

When this fixed Water Sign chooses to hitch on their daily mysterious ride, they'd rather take it solo. Many become offended by their need to be observant, quiet, and often times alone. These characteristics are not meant to hurt anyone. Scorpio sees little validity in sharing what they experience internally. Their thinking is: "What would you do with the information I express to you? Hold it against me at a later date? I'll keep the hidden jewels to myself, until I know it is imperative to express myself." Scorpio energy prides itself on respecting sacred information, and its ability to share what it chooses. When they decide to share, don't take it lightly. It takes a tremendous amount of courage for them to trust anyone with the depths of their emotions. However, when this rare occurrence happens, they remain devoted to their passion and never waiver from the convictions of what they stand for.

I've always been a lover of words. I'm fascinated by the imagery, the feelings, and the inspiration you receive when you read novels and re-live powerful passages of poetry. I've been writing poems since I was ten years old and possess fifty-five journals to date. These scribes describe my surroundings and venting frustrations while adding vivid colors to an existence where they were sometimes absent. The power of the word has literally changed my life. Little did I know, my talents would afford me a chance to be a featured poet on a multi-platinum soundtrack, "Waiting to Exhale", land a recording contract with LaFace Records, and receive a publishing deal with EMI Music Publishing in the early '90s. This incredible experience allowed me to travel, and work with and meet wildly talented individuals such as Whitney Houston, Toni Braxton, and Usher Raymond, just to name a few. At the time, I made more money than I'd ever experienced. It was cool to be twenty-four years old and admitted into parties I wouldn't normally attend, while developing relationships with musical icons, such as Teena Marie.

I was riding high for two years, exploring uncharted territory no one in my family had ever seen. However, this adventure quickly turned daunting. I had no prior knowledge or understanding of the business of music, and like many new artists I was misinformed by the glamour, yet lack of reality, the industry's "celebrity" presented. First, you must have an honest and respected lawyer and legal team to keep your finances and contracts in order. It's imperative to protect yourself and future earnings, in order to steer clear of tax troubles or personal economic confusion later in life. Second, the entertainment industry has a persuasive undertow that can pull you into addictions, power trips, illegal dealings, and inauthenticity many rather not talk about. I've witnessed executives take advantage of up and coming singers and songwriters, use their power as leverage to receive what they want (i.e. sexual favors), and shelve projects because of the company's inability to recognize the artists' creative intentions. It's sad to watch a young adult's hopes and dreams be manipulated by a select few, whose only interest is to capitalize on their gifts. I became resistant to these ways when asked to market my poetry/musical project through the interpretation of jazz. I love jazz, but the hip-hop culture is bred in my soul. I wanted to create music that was representative of who I was at the time. I wished to write about subject matters that young adults were plagued with, such as lack of self-love and the abuse of capitalism in underprivilege neighborhoods.

Needless to say, they thought my words were too introspective for a market they believed was only interested in sex and irresponsible celebration. When I was asked to wear certain clothes that didn't resonate with my moral judgement, I refused. When my family and friends saw these adjustments as minor sacrifices and opportunities I should swallow for the bigger picture, I utilized a Scorpio's viewpoint and saw these as poor intrinsic decisions for my future. My desire to explore a deeper meaning of my life and its purpose didn't allow me to comprise. I journeyed past the superficial rewards of money and fame by writing poetry that reflected my inner thoughts, and the rejection of the unjust dealings of others.

Within a year of getting signed, I lost my contract with LaFace Records. The record industry was losing money at the time, due to the exploding developments of the internet, and I was told they no longer wanted to nurture an artist who could potentially be a headache because of my truths and adverse viewpoints I was willing to share through my poetry. I was devastated. I wanted to bring light and understanding to everything I envisioned unfair. The depths of my thinking needed to be exposed, but not alongside power hungry crooks or misogynistic marketing plans. In retrospect, I would do it the same way all over again, if I could. I changed the course of my life based on my convictions, my unknown. The depths of my creed exposed the importance of standing my ground, instead of emerging as an older adult who couldn't live with her previous decisions. A lot of my peers became addicted to drugs or acquired massive debt; I believe as a result being someone they were forced to be. Looking past the obvious allowed me to dodge those outcomes and remain rooted in the wisdom of my poetry that propelled me at ten years old. Our talents and gifts belong to us, and examining the purpose of fortitude, forged on by an innate Scorpio energy, may allow us to dodge several deceptive bullets. Staying true to the unseen magic we possess allows us to remain true to the gifts we are innately blessed with by our Creator.

Scorpio energy operates like a powerful surge of sensory conviction. While observing more than the average person, they have a way of decoding hidden emotions and desires undetected by others. They know exactly how a person should be spoken to and sensually touched, because they pay close attention to unseen body language that displays cravings or desires unknown to most. Many interpret Scorpio energy as being highly sexual by nature. Although it may appear true, it's deeper than that. Scorpios present a wondrous, enigmatic energy that was created to probe beyond the confines of another's heart and mind, in an effort to unlock any hidden desires another may find difficult to articulate. This elusive energy can be found in inanimate objects, as well. When was the last time you let a red light glaring in your bedroom hypnotize you? Or, let someone hover over you without touching you? The vibrations streaming forth is reminiscent of this sign finding its way to your core without your permission. Scorpio people are determined to physically please a partner through imagination and sensory control. Oftentimes, we carry personal baggage that can prohibit ultimate, sexual pleasures; those with this sun sign have a plan for that. A Scorpio state of passion allows us to free ourselves and enjoy connections with others as creatures of a divine experience extending past the obvious. This sign wishes to reintroduce us to the essence of creation, the power of intimacy that has birthed us all. Scorpio energy says, "Surrender, and trust the process." It dares you to meet a side of yourself that could ignite a life spun from your inner sanctions, rather than enduring life from the limited confines of your superficial world. Music has a way of sandblasting any personal armor we carry. Not too many would argue with me when I say that the following artist is a master of manipulating the senses with the power of sound, vibrations, and allure.

The compelling energy of the musical genius, Prince, has seduced millions. He emerged on the music scene leaving spectators in awe of his multiple instrument playing abilities, dynamic lyrics, and incomparable vocal skills. However, it was his unknown, sexual persuasion that seized the attention of most. Never revealing too much about his private life in interviews, he left you on the brink of the unknown to wonder, "Who is this dude?" He exhibited masculine and feminine ways through his style of dress, and unique visual presentations. Ambiguous in nature, yet passionate in delivery, we were all brought to the edge of his sensual explorations. The bass lines in some songs sparked lustful urges that were relentless and unyielding, the choice of words was descriptive, raw, and colorful, and the melodies he chose sounded like sweet pleas of love and delight whispered softly in your ear. Fans were willing to go on an unknown ride as his piercing eyes led the way, and his sheepish, yet sexy glances made you slightly uneasy and wanting more. He presented an undertow of passion that propelled our sexual drive and compelled our hearts to open and surrender untouched gifts. Prince was wildly creative and successfully persuasive. Anyone who experienced a live show can honestly say they visited a land that's difficult to return from. It smelled of freedom, experimentation, fun, and abandonment. It pushed beyond the status quo of what sexual exploration "should" look like and created a vision of its own. He was one of the best forces that urged his listeners to discover new ways to ignite any and all hidden desires. Prince's Scorpio ascendant energy struck us deep in our feelings, until it was time to come out and meet the "real world" again. From the depths of our emotions to the light of the evident, this sign is always willing to foster an exciting ride.

Scorpio energy can be akin to the unpredictability of a seemingly calm, serene lake. One moment you are gazing at its unbothered yet mysterious outer appearance, and the next moment you are thrown into the undercurrent of its determined drive, leaving those around it feeling shocked and bewildered. This contrasting existence keeps Scorpio energy moving forward, and creating life based on instantaneous decisions that plow it forward toward a desired destination. Scorpio energy works well with the conviction of the extreme; all or nothing, zero to sixty. When sparked by purpose and the necessity to see a project through, Scorpios easily attract the right people to assist in their quest. This sign magically manifests what it needs, based on passionate will and conviction. Scorpio energy usually initiates this surge due to boredom. Moved by a state of mind that's "played out", or a seemingly unhealthy circumstance, it immediately springs in another direction. It becomes relentless to succeed when a way of life doesn't serve their "highest good" or better judgement. Scorpios thrive on pulling information and courage from any unknown source to create something bigger, better, and more suitable to travel towards an entirely new destination. A Scorpio's determination is single focused and cutthroat, if need be; nothing will stand in between them and victory. This type of energy was definitely needed during a time in history when Nancy Regan's plea to "just say no" was slightly overdue. Many inner-city youth, living within the throws of addiction, sought to make a better life for themselves through sheer, radical change.

The '80s was a decadent decade that produced electronic music production, and drugs that were designed to destroy people. Crack was a cheap derivative of cocaine, which operated as a hyper hallucinogenic. It rotted the brain, took your appetite, made you violent (in some cases), and snatched you away from anything that felt like love. It's usage usually left you desolate and penniless, or at the least robbed you of any dignity you possessed. It was an awful experience watching childhood friends and family members become victims to its destruction. I recall the summer of 1984. It began with my friends and I as rowdy teenagers in Yonkers, NY, drinking beers and smoking weed. Unfortunately, the summer ended with half the neighborhood drifting away from our previous activities to sneaking behind buildings to do things I wasn't permitted to partake in. I was never, ever interested in crack! Unfortunately, that wasn't the case for millions of lost souls. I had a friend, we'll call her Donna, who enjoyed the euphoria more than our regular crew. Within six months, she was kicked out of the house, became pregnant, and was hooked on crack as a daily habit. Donna began petty criminal activity, which led her to rehab and jail. It was one of the most heart-wrenching things to witness. A brilliant teenager, with dreams of becoming a doctor, turned into a young adult who battled her inner fears with the help of crack cocaine. Selfish choices designed a virtual "hell on earth", and in the eyes of many Donnas, she looked like a hopeless case that would fall victim to inevitable death.

However, the power of rebirth and determination, prompted by Scorpio energy, found its way to her. My friend was determined to reinvent herself and live a life contrary to what she experienced prior to doing jail time. An awakening propelled her to utilize her God given gifts, and cease wasting valuable time. She became hungry for success in ways she never thought she could achieve in her darkest days. She redirected the destruction she created, with the same intensity, towards positive steps that assured an abundant future. Donna surrendered to an unknown outcome by falling into a life she knew nothing about, in order to develop into her best self. Her 180-degree turn began with going to night school and achieving a Bachelor of Arts degree in Business. She then held three jobs and worked her way through the ranks to become a current supervisor in her field. She rose like the phoenix out of the ashes of destruction and imminent death to discover the strength and the brilliance she was destined to have. Today, she's making over $100,000 a year, with a host of responsibilities that include being the matriarch of her family. She has triumphed through the darkest years of her existence to tell the story and be an example. This is the power of Scorpio energy! Its resilience will turn a volcanic eruption into the most glorious field of lilies for all to see.

When you examine the powerful surge of Scorpio energy, you can learn to use it to your advantage. It urges you to be a powerful force that ignores the fears and apprehensions of the world, in order to create new experiences. Scorpios lead with a stubborn conviction like no other. They pull strength from areas in their being that leave many baffled and bewildered. Although their mysterious nature may seem cunning and secretive at times, it's only meant to shield their deep emotions and sensitive soul. This sign's energy highlights the urgency to change, and the power to destroy anything that needs rebuilding.

Questions for the Scorpio in you:

What would you gain in life if you trusted the ways of the world, just a little more?

How do you plan to transform boring, destructive areas of your life into brilliant masterpieces?

How can you persuade a mate to feel the power of love, instead of the expectancy of "good sex"?

What's the healthiest way to exercise your devotion without sacrificing yourself?

Haniel's Corner:

Dear Scorpio, your energy is necessary in a world that promises to present setbacks in our evolution, through greed and insensitivity. We live in a society that prides itself on dismantling truth and implementing fabricated ways that raise us with conditions. You seek to destroy this notion through awareness, courage, and a determination to live according to one's own design. Your intensity should not be ridiculed, but rather celebrated for seeing pass the norm and encouraging change and passion. Scorpio remember to care about the plight of humanity, and quietly defend it with devotion and loyalty like the front line of any military brigade. Use your emotional strength to be willing to pick up the pieces of life and start all over again, while craftily intuiting the next step. You know life never ends; it's a continuous cycle of reinvention through faithful actions and activation of one's senses to be born again and again.

Mantra

"I trust the waves of passion will carry me where I need to be, with grace and simplicity."

CHAPTER NINE

⊷⃝⊶

SAGITTARIUS – The Seeker

"I am a steady flame of hope burning threats of despair;
an honest beacon of light - so blunt, so cavalier.
Freedom marks the destination I relentlessly obtain.
In the meantime, I bring the party...again and again and again!"

"Everything is going to be alright!" is the mantra of Sagittarius people. Using optimism as its superpower, coupled with never-ending physical energy, they tirelessly find a solution to any problem presented. This fire sign contains an abundance of resources, and useful information that it proudly shares with anyone willing to listen. Getting to the bottom of a dilemma or, at the very least, pointing you in the direction of someone who might, is always a priority of theirs. It pains a Sag to see someone in distress when they know they have enough information to provide a quick fix. The daily goal of this sign is for everyone in their environment to stay happy and satisfied. The Archer has a zest for life many consider naive or lucky. Pulling proverbial rabbits out of a hat, at the eleventh hour, is a regular occurrence, rarely fretting and always believing that life will hand you exactly what you need. They wildly commit to this characteristic, so they may avoid pain and discomfort. Floating on "a wing and a prayer" is the optimum form of transportation through their journey of life. They'd rather over commit, and loosely promise you the world, before they give you any indication something cannot be achieved. Although they are not strangers to getting their hands dirty, using the concept of disciplined, hard work often constitutes as their last resort. According to the ninth Sign of the Zodiac, it's less strenuous to use their upbeat charm and idealistic confidence, then work their fingers to the bone, when achieving a goal. Everything is done with ease, as long as everyone is playing by their rules.

When life is orchestrated by a wand of lighthearted joyousness, freedom is promoted. Given the space to make mistakes, to learn as they go, and to convince a select few that they are more intrinsic then they really are contributes to the formula of Sags achieving the impossible dream. Imagine the hopeful vitality in the eyes of a high school graduate, or an eager employee on the first day of their dream job. You're face-to-face with the essence of Sag energy. Any experience in life that combines a strong belief system with a desire to learn more is indicative of the Archer. True liberation is paramount when allowing their soul, the autonomy to choose their life experiences, rather than another enforcing alternative outlooks that don't seem to resonate with them. Simply put, Sags detest being controlled. Like an untamed stallion, dancing unabashedly in the wind, they allow the elements of existence to carry them assuredly through time and space. As long as the path is led with truth and nobility, in a way that benefits its choices, this energy is devoted to any worthwhile cause. Sagittarian energy focuses on the bigger picture and the end result. It may not have a detailed plan as to how it will get there, but the destination always remains in clear view. Sag optimism is the catalyst that carries them wherever they desire. Personally, I've tapped into this fire sign's vibration often, especially during the times when I was "finding myself" and searching for projects and small purposes that left an indelible stain on whatever I touched. Sag energy helped me to discover my talents with joy, void of regrets.

In 1988, I entered Hampton University, a prestigious HBCU (historically Black college and university) located in Hampton, VA. As a pre-med major, I toted accelerated dreams of becoming the first physician in my family. I love animals and children, so either veterinary medicine or pediatrics was going to be my end game. It felt like a natural fit. My mom was widely known and endeared as one of the best nurses New York State had encountered. People flocked to experience her care. She was always kind, considerate, and professional with every patient she encountered. I wished to make her proud and take her legacy one step further as a doctor. However, after enrolling in Botany during the second semester of my freshman year, I fell out of love with the dream of carrying the torch. The study of plants bored me to death, and science began to kill an important part of my life, my creativity. My zeal for magic, production, colors, and song, that I'd learned to appreciate in my early years, started to dwindle and I suddenly became consumed by formulas and facts that dulled my senses, So, I switched majors. I called my mom one random Tuesday evening, and eagerly announced, "I am changing my emphasis of study to Theater Arts and Speech Communication."

"WHAT?" she asked, shocked. "What the hell are you going to do with a Theater degree?"

Honestly, I didn't have an answer. I barely had a plan for what I was going to eat the next day. All I knew was that my intuitive hunches never steered me wrong, and it was my job to remain positively hopeful that this decision would lead me to my destiny. Becoming a doctor was a noble and somewhat obligatory task I set out to achieve, but the arts, the word, and the flare of fantasy and imagination sparked my heart and soul; I had to oblige. I jumped into a life-changing decision with the strength and conviction I found along my journey. My optimism paved the way, void of a strategy most parents would like their children to implement. A sudden ownership of my life was scary to my mom, at first, but she eased into the notion after small bouts of success followed my decision. I became the number one radio deejay at WHOV,88.3 FM, Hampton University's radio station, and became a notable lighting designer and director for several theatrical productions at HU.

The four years I spent receiving my undergraduate degree were some of the most rewarding years of my life. A new path was carved out in front of me - a path no one in my family had ever travelled. It matured me greatly. The tenacity and determination I possessed through stressful times left me proud, and confident that I was able to survive on my own. I held several jobs to assist with my financial responsibilities, a few teachers were enlisted as spiritual advisors to keep me focused on my goals, and I successfully navigated social freedom and pressures that aimed to steer me from my academic responsibilities. I basked in the Sagittarius moniker of positivity and employed it to lead the way. It was risky, but well worth the chance. I found happiness and contentment in living my truth in a bold and honest way.

Sagittarius energy prides itself on honesty. Of course, Sags have told a few fabricated tales, however, showing integrity when presenting a true account of who they are always remains essential. When a Sag expresses their truth, an expectation is created; always relate to them according to what's told, and never rely on speculations. They seek clarity by abolishing secrets and hidden agendas within their experiences. Respect is garnered when you treat them the same. If another's feelings happen to be affected by their candor, it's never intentional. It's simply a form of true expression, so there's no question as to where they stand. With this in mind, Sagittarians can also suffer from "foot in mouth disease"- an affliction of saying what's on their minds too quickly, void of compassion. This sign believes emotions are separate from the doctrine of truth. Honesty is a gallant act that aims to fortify a connection, not destroy it with personal sensitivities. According to the Sagittarius sun sign, one should be considered honored to experience such sincerity in their presence. It opens the door for stress-free relationships. Always flashing honesty as a badge of honor also allows them to heal from traumatic situations. Many seem to relax into the acceptance of hard truth and often times begin a quest to find what's relatable. Thus, a "life-saving" sense of humor is erected. Whenever you sense an honest mistake in yourself or another, an alternative reaction may ask you to chuckle, accept your shortcomings, and emerge on the other side of pain. You begin to see it wasn't that serious to begin with. According to Sagittarius energy, it never was.

Sagittarius energy relies on its easily accessible form of humor. Comedy is a Sag's secret weapon and is used to cut through agitations and negativity to expose their truths, all while keeping others happy. They find humor in the most unlikely places, aimed to destroy a potential panic of "something's wrong". This brand of humor puts everything on the table, so to speak, and breaks past any embarrassment or inability to completely dismiss how painful a situation may have been. Some of the greatest comedians within the last fifty years have a strong influence of Sagittarian energy. Richard Pryor, Flip Wilson, Redd Foxx, and John Stewart, just to name a few, have utilized the art of getting to the core of an issue, and making fun of themselves before anyone else can. One thing they all have in common is the ability to turn hardships into stories of hope, and unfortunate circumstances into common denominators we may all share.

Richard Pryor was born in Peoria, IL, and raised in a brothel by his beloved grandmother. He experienced many unfortunate conditions- from poverty to addiction, from prostitution to violence. Since his mother was a prostitute, and his father was absent most of his life, he wasn't nurtured the way children deserve. Unfortunately, reports of sexual abuse as a youngster attributed to him developing an extremely unruly reputation in school. Richard continuously found trouble and fighting his way out of any situation was routine. He lived on the defense; he caressed the edge. In true Sagittarius fashion, however, he learned to use comedy as a way to express his grievances and give voice to the bleak circumstances handed to him. He became more vulnerable with his comedic material and used his platform as a cathartic way to express his ill-fated relationships, drug dependencies, and racist and sexist experiences. His raw accounts of life won audiences over. They could relate to his reality; as they saw themselves in him, or they witnessed it in another's life close to them. Richard Pryor had an uncanny way of presenting harsh truths in your face to knock off the blinders, and spawn "real" dialogue based on distressed personal issues many allow to mount in their lives. Even though he was most noted for his success in the film industry, he was famously recognized for redirecting his memories into imagination and prosperity during his stand-up act. This form of comedy opened the door for many aspiring comedians to take a similar route. Dave Chappelle and Eddie Murphy are examples of comedians that adopted Richard Pryor's immense courage. He inadvertently acted as a teacher and mentor of his craft, urging others to heal by exposing their unique narratives.

When you feel the need to teach and share throughout the world, in any capacity, you have Sagittarian energy to thank. The desire to learn and pass on information to rightfully inform another is an innate desire of Sag energy. It is a passion for the Archer to gather resources via books, websites, and experts in a given field, and openly assist another to receive a better understanding of any subject. This sign believes in the expansion of knowledge and allowing new information to shape different thought patterns and viewpoints within a potential student. According to a Sag, learning is equivalent to adventure- the act of adding more to your arsenal of life's experiences and growing fully within your current incarnation by receiving information others may not be privy to. They believe part of their purpose is to consider their penchant for travel abroad and ask bold questions of unfamiliar cultures, philosophies, and belief systems. Even though they may not always be welcomed, as they probe with inquiry, it never matters. According to them, rejection is included in the process of being intrigued. Sagittarians understand that one must utilize determination, at all costs, to receive what's necessary to evolve and demonstrate their findings. Although they have the energy and wherewithal to obtain knowledge, they find it arduous, and sometimes boring, when it calls for them to apply structure and discipline in order to receive results. They'd rather instruct someone else to handle the information and be done with it. Providing knowledge as an act of service is a lot more suitable for their nature. Sagittarius energy usually gathers and shares and offers a non-judgmental space to learn and grow. The library, one of my favorite places on the planet, seems to be indicative of that energy, and a place to safely get lost in information while following the rabbit hole into unknown islands in the South Pacific. Another example would be a sacred place I grew to love and happened to be an establishment created by someone close to me.

A dear friend of mine, Moneek, owned a quaint boutique in the downtown section of Pasadena, CA called, Kafe Sol. (She currently runs a shop similar to this in Atlanta, Ga. called, Sanktuari) It housed beautiful spiritual tools such as tarot cards, prayer infused candles, and gemstone jewelry. Traditional African garments and well-constructed djembe drums lined the walls proudly, and there was always a scent of East Indian incense caressing the air. Many Friday nights were spent immersing ourselves in the energy of our ancestors, thrusted in the center of drum circles and African dance classes of all ages. My peers and I attended many lectures on women's health, parenting, and maintaining successful relationships. The exchanges created an insatiable appetite within me to add to the scene and share what I knew - the intuitive art of Western Astrology.

Sometime in the 2000s, Moneek invited me to conduct my first Western Astrology workshop in her beautiful boutique. By all accounts, I was nervous as heck. In the back of my mind, I fretted over how I would successfully convey a vast metaphysical science within a three-hour time period. Would people walk away more confused than they arrived? Would I forget any important points that could assist in their knowledge of themselves? I hoped I wouldn't bore them to death. I spent hours upon hours gathering information that would make it easier for my students to devour the information. I thought to use suitable analogies and personal examples to make the information easily digestible. Much like Sagittarius energy, I used my excitement as a way of dispensing knowledge without concentrating on a detailed outline. I focused on utilizing everyday life experiences to create visuals and reference points for my first-time students, displaying copious amounts of fervor, humor, and my down-to-earth New York realism. On numerous occasions during the workshop, I would forget to slow down when I talked, and take account of who was absorbing the information. My excitement overshadowed any organizational skills; I just wanted to share. It made me overjoyed to observe the twinkle in another's eyes when astrology made sense to a stranger. My heart did flips in my chest as I watched tears roll down the faces of my new clients/students, simply by using the proverbial mirror of Western Astrology to reflect truths, closer than they imagined. Even today, there's not enough money in the world I would take in exchange for that feeling. Helping someone evolve, based on the willingness to give, is what humanity is about. There's overwhelming joy in assisting others with tools to fly.

Sagittarius energy pervades our planet with contagious optimism. It begs us to pay close attention to the strength and determination we have to evolve beyond our perceived ceiling of life and asks that we get lost in the freedom of music and laughter. Sagittarius energy opens your heart to explore past the confines of an often restricting and critical society. Learn from its freedom and bask in its hope. It's infectious, forgiving, and divine, and always remains wide-eyed for the magic of life…until the road has found its end.

Questions to ask the Sagittarius in you:

When you assist another with learning important information, do you follow up to see how it serviced them?

Have you let the power of laughter destroy the pain you once felt, only to emerge feeling victorious and shrugging your shoulders to any remnants of despair?

Have you ever ended an emotional bond with someone, because their actions seemed to threaten your freedom?

Has your optimistic nature blinded you from seeing the truth in another person, or situation?

Haniel's Corner:

Dear Sagittarius, your energy is responsible for maintaining a lighthearted nature in a world that would rather feed fear and the appearance of control. Many conservative people find challenging the norm with harsh truths, offensive. When necessary, you forge your own path with delight, optimism, generosity, and hope. Incorporating a secret desire for all to get along may be the truth you rarely discuss. Reserve the right to agree to disagree and be mindful not to impose your truth on another. Everyone discovers and growth at their own pace. Many may even condemn your seemingly irresponsible, overly optimistic way of living. It's not your problem. Inject your bouts of happiness wherever you land, while always remaining respectable of others space and time.

Mantra:

"I use freedom as a way of creating my life exactly as I see fit."

CHAPTER TEN

⤜ت⤛

CAPRICORN – The Achiever

"I will stop at nothing to see a dream realized.
No problem can stunt my growth; no victory will leave me satisfied.
Life is not worth living if there's no mountain to climb."

Capricorn energy is born "on a mission". It's an ambitious force created to conquer any puzzling scheme with an intense discipline other zodiac signs may take lifetimes to decipher. This earth sign gets the job done! It has a unique approach to winning, however, as it first identifies what doesn't work, in order to recognize what does work. This initial step may seem extremely pessimistic, to most, as they initially look for the explosive mines in the minefield that will impede on success. This strategy works best for the tenth Sign of the Zodiac. They love to weed out the weakest link by identifying the competition who pose a threat. Ambition feeds a Capricorn's competitive edge and provides knowledge of unknown tactics that ensure they continue to win everything they encounter. Imagine an inspiring football player attending every NFL game he could; sitting high in the bleachers to watch brilliant plays as well as the mistakes, only to study how to "be better". It's a diligence only Capricorn energy exhibits. They believe in chomping at the bit, one step at a time, following plans and provisions that are practical by nature. Have you ever seen a goat scale an incline? Its hooves balance on the smallest edge for hours, while contemplating its next move. Watching them maneuver is a science many cannot grasp. They plan and scheme, and manipulate resources and people, in order to obtain what they need. It is never a personal attack or a selfish move; the idea is to utilize what's available and allow their slow and steady climb to count.

Capricorn energy is tenacious, and slightly self-righteous, when proving its brilliance. They pride themselves on remaining moral and just in whatever task they're involved in, always giving reverence to traditions and rituals that have been passed down from generation to generation. Capricorn energy finds delight in utilizing tools and familial information, in an effort to maintain the foundation they were built on. If they cannot win with a proven form of integrity, then there was never a "real" contest to begin with. Rules are important, and certain conventions must be upheld to establish substance and stability during times of uncertainty. If you really want to see a Capricorn working its magic, pay attention to the one who's always looking through the rule book during family game night. They are hell bent in ensuring everyone wins fairly, otherwise your victory doesn't count and you're immoral in their eyes. This sign is a leader by nature, willing to delegate commands, but more than capable of handling the task alone. Capricorn energy prides itself on executing a plan to joyfully see a project to the end. More importantly, the experience garners wisdom that assists another person in conquering the same goal. What would the world be like if Capricorn energy didn't share its findings, or spend sleepless nights hard at work to prime all of us for victory? Whether it's for the group or a personal quest, Capricorns utilize ritual and the art of repetition to demonstrate what they're made of. I stepped into this arena, once or twice, led by the devotion of Capricorn energy, and trusted that the steps I made would lead me exactly where I wanted to be.

Fasting has become a common ritual of mine over the past twenty years. It initially started as a way to lose weight and cleanse my body of unwanted toxins. However, it has developed into a personal ritual that leaves me feeling accomplished and victorious, even when life becomes challenging. I've participated in many different types of fasts: all vegetables, just fruit, no sugar, and even a few verbal fasts. The latter was done to heighten my keen sense of observation. It enabled me to pay closer attention to what people were REALLY saying. I often found that people talk to hear themselves profess knowledge out loud, which ultimately serves their ego and disregards the importance of the listener's input. For them, the art of communication – listening to understand rather than hearing to respond – becomes insignificant over the years.

One of my most memorable fasts was an all liquid, twenty-one day fast. I disciplined myself to drink only liquids for a daily, allotted time frame in order to clear my mind, remove myself of any toxins, and strengthen my will power for future achievements. The first three to five days proved to be the most challenging. Your body is essentially starving itself of nutrients and the pleasurable foods it's used to. As long as you remain dedicated, this part of the process will handle itself. My stomach shrank, and after the fifth day, I was no longer famished. The real challenge came within the next week to ten days, when life moved forward as planned, and I was invited to dinner and happy hour after work. Socially, I remained involved with life, but I couldn't partake in the obvious pleasures. I once read a quote from a guru, famously known for fasting: "You receive the blessings from fasting when you sit at the table to eat, and know you are there to partake in nourishing your soul rather than your stomach." It always makes sense after the fact, but during the practice I would have gladly eaten a napkin to soothe my urge to swallow something solid. The novelty wore off after I'd explained fifty-five times, to strangers and family, why I was conducting this mind altering, body challenging event in the first place. Days 10 to 15, there was no reason to explain, and there was no need to talk. I would awake knowing I had to put my "head down" within this grueling process, and get the job done. I questioned my motives and need to put my body through this nearly impossible task that made a French fry look like a gourmet meal. During the final days of fasting, the personal contest became equivalent to the twenty third mile in a marathon. Capricorn's energy within me, and its will to succeed, wouldn't allow me to quit after going so far, but I definitely found it excruciating to continue. On Day 15, I decided to give myself something to look forward to. I began watching cooking shows that offered new recipes for exciting, exotic dishes - the kind I would I never, in a million years, attempt to recreate. Oddly enough, this helped ease my senses, and satisfied the pleasure triggers I refused to feed. The artist in me was excited and grateful for the inspiration. I was like the goat scaling a mountain and overjoyed to find a steady step. The visual perspective was gratifying, and seemingly all I required in those moments. The last five days revealed the reward. I no longer had the desire to eat, nor was I irritated by a sense of lack. I was lucid and full of energy, almost as if I was surviving off the air. The sensation of almost achieving this feat left me feeling extremely euphoric, and spiritually gratified.

At the time, I was writing songs and performing locally. Every gig felt like I had ascended through the clouds, and every musical note reverberated deep within my bones. This was the prize of discipline, the bounty of will. I utilized the steadfast, ambitious energy of Capricorn to catapult me to a mountain peak I didn't know existed and was rewarded with an intense knowing of being capable of doing anything. I won't fast for twenty-one days again, but I'm blessed to share my experiences to encourage the next pioneering soul.

One of the most important ingredients for a Capricorn's stride is the ability to remain in control of their own destiny. As children, they were usually serious and to-the-point when mounting any challenge and navigating solely by themselves. They constantly enlisted the assistance of those they held in high regard to offer the best advice, only to alter the instructions to cater to their own procedures. Any slight alterations will allow Capricorn energy jurisdiction over its leadership, regardless if it succeeds or fails. A sharp sense of responsibility is then born out of the need to remain in power and have an opinion on every aspect of its job, personal life, or another's life (if permitted). When a Capricorn's insights are shared and implemented, waves of pride and self-admiration follow. There is a deep-seated and frequently overlooked sensitivity that lurks within these "boss" types. The unseen aspect of this sign's emotions is the catalyst behind making sure any task is completed closest to perfection. Spawned by a caring yet direct heart, Caps may seem cold when leading with dominance. Contrarily, they have a masked desire to please people and facilitate exactly what they need. To surrender to the intelligence, influence, or hunches of anyone else is comparable to a person with a fear of bugs camping in the wilderness overnight. It's a dangerous step outside of their comfort zone, yielding themselves to the unknown- a sure indication that a situation will not go well, in comparison to their "best plan". According to the Goat, all preparations done by them are fool proof. Hours and days of research create success, from their pragmatic viewpoint. Hard work and diligence give them license to be in authority. It's only right that their idea is best after they put in optimum strength and effort.

Capricorn energy is masterful in controlling itself, and always poised in position with polite and diplomatic responses that offer respect and reverence at all times. They never want to appear to be "taken off their square." Permitting another to see their vulnerability creates holes in their character they are not willing to explain. Caps would rather you see them the way in which "they" decide. It protects their heart and keeps them focused on managing their achievements. Controlling any and all aspects of their lives puts the attention on more impeding issues of the world. In some ways, this helps to preserve the integrity and enlightenment of the entire collective. The thought is, "I'll take care of myself, while we manage together and adhere to outside circumstances." I suspect a number of celebrities aspire to achieve this outlook, but I've only witnessed one who has done it quite successfully.

My first introduction to Leonardo DiCaprio was his powerful performance in "Basketball Diaries". It tells an urban tale of a high school basketball player who becomes addicted to heroin. He was extremely captivating, embodying the emotional capacity needed to portray such a wounded character at such a young age. I thought, "He's about to become the next Clark Gable, or Tom Hanks. A celebrated actor, winning awards and receiving notable acclaim. Wildly popular among teenagers and adults alike, shooting his star of fame straight to his apex, without a moment to pause." You often see these types of celebrities come and go. Seemingly, they get a taste of more money than they've ever imagined and spend it frivolously under the guise of opulence and privilege. Some might even lose their composure by embodying characters they portray and convince themselves they're the invincible "bad guy" that will never be held responsible for their childish outbursts in real life. To my knowledge, Leonardo never journeyed down this road.

He became involved with notable projects that displayed depth and celebrated wild creativity. Sure, the movie, "Titanic", was a blockbuster that put him on the map. However, with that success, he seemed to do more for climate change and spoke on the behalf of serving humanity. Many movies followed that seemed to challenge the artist he was becoming. "Inception" and "The Revenant" pushed the envelope of our imagination through mental acrobatics and bending physical limits. Leonardo encapsulated the vibration of Capricorn energy by controlling his narrative. He choreographed his success with a body of work he could be proud of. The guidance of Cap energy inspired him to control the direction of his legacy by choosing projects and professionals to work with that have a sense of purpose, and a need to shine light on important subject matters. Bravo, sir!

Capricorn energy is keenly aware of the concept of the "tried and true." The blanket that brings you comfort, your grandfather's tailored smoking jacket, and Sunday dinners with the family sharing stories around the table, all bring a sense of normalcy and familiarity to Capricorn energy. Order and structure bring balance to an already chaotic world. Traditions spawn pride when instilling history, character, and wisdom that keep a family mended in the midst of disjointed, social "norms". A connection to family and values that will never be broken are key. Frequently, this is created through rituals that are passed down, such as going to church every Sunday or making a honey and ginger concoction that soothes a wound on your skin. These formalities bring pride to a Capricorn's heart, and are shared with generations to come. This sentiment is slightly patriarchal in nature, as well, headed by a leader who assuredly shares the details of how to receive ease through a remedy made sixty years ago. Structure and detail add reverence to rituals, and honor to their inception. Capricorns love to notice a "government" in place, regarding any area in their lives. When it comes to family life, they prefer that every member has a job and a duty to assist the entire clan. When these jobs and tasks are performed diligently, ritual is created, and the fulfillment of love is inevitable.

My paternal grandmother, Grandma Jo, attempted to create a ritual for me during my young years. Being an awesome cook and baker, she attempted to teach me how to prepare classic dishes that have been in our family for generations. I just wanted to laugh with her, look at her pretty hands and nails, and listen to albums from the stereo/bar component she owned. I would show her the new dances and sing every song, word for word. Un-knowingly, we were creating a ritual of our own, and received an injection of joy and good food during these priceless moments. Apparently, she had other intentions of creating rituals during this time and aspired to teach me to cook. I started out on chopping and cutting duty - always asked to mince garlic, and cube red onions and potatoes.

However, I longed to be on spice detail. Learning how flavors engaged each other, tasting what was missing (and what she used too much of) in a dish, was my aspiration. I wanted to cook like her so badly, but I admit I was too young and impatient to engage in the ritual she presented. Cooking like her required a rhythm and a dance that taught you how to finesse food, and pour love into beans, cheeses, and meat. My grandmother used to blurt out in a quiet moment, "A good cook is a clean cook!" That was a signal to wash the dishes she placed in the sink, wipe off the counter tops for the next batch of biscuits, or take out the trash to make room in the kitchen for more trash. She unknowingly created a ceremony of sorts; flavors, music, utensils, and smiles. The repetition of these moments cemented memories in my heart that will resonate throughout my entire life. It produced a need to share moments like these with my son. I cannot cook as well as her, because I never graduated from cutting duties, but I can show him how to precisely dice a clove of garlic. No ritual is too small, and no duty is too minor. Even after she has soared onto to Heaven, I am proud to be the cleanest sous chef in town.

We have Capricorn energy to thank for precious moments we tend to overlook. Many of its influences look serious and regimented in nature, but it always proves to be reliable, structured, ordered, and disciplined - only aiming to establish honor to its character. Without it, the entire foundation of life could potentially crumble and cave in.

Time to pay close attention to the structures that keep us moving forward in life, give them honor, and share your findings. Thanks to Capricorn energy, we'll all have moments that keep us rising to the top.

Questions to ask the Capricorn in you:

What familial traditions do you consciously adhere to, on a daily basis, to keep you focused and cemented in your steps to personal success?

When was the last time you delegated duties at home, or work, without micromanagement?

When was the last time you went to a party exclusively for fun, without thoughts of work or ambitious thoughts attached to it?

What was the last person, situation, or outcome you tried to control, and failed to do so?

Haniel's Corner:

Dear Capricorn, be wary of staying stuck in your structured life. Although you're needed to plan and construct a path for movements far bigger than you, Spirit needs your perseverance and resolve to distribute tradition and order to the masses. It doesn't need you to strong-arm results or control any personal outcomes. Surrender your innate duties to the powers that be when you reach your limit and remember to take time to play. Understand that life is not that serious, and nothing will fall apart if you step away from your post for five minutes. Honestly, you tend to get younger as you get older, so live life as the adventure it was intended to be. Thank goodness we have your energy and your plan to lean on if we lose our way.

Mantra:

"I concede my power to something greater than me when I am no longer in control. It knows my hearts desires better than I do."

CHAPTER ELEVEN

AQUARIUS – The Original

"There is no one like me, I guarantee.
My vision extends beyond trends, because I'm the next best thing.
Slightly arrogant yet, a rebel in boots.
…Stomping out fires for humanity."

The words of one of my favorite rhythm and blues/funk bands, Cameo,

"She's strange…,and I like it!" best describes the unique disposition of the Water Bearer. Aquarius is an insurgent soul, deposited on the planet Earth to make massive changes just by being themselves. They have no inclination to follow suit or, live their lives like a replica of anyone they've met. Aquarian energy is unique in thinking, being, dressing, and acting. Everything about this Air sign energy is "left of center", and they love it that way. Normal is boring, and conservatism chokes their creativity and zest for life. Their original way of thinking is welcomed by most, due to the friendly disposition with which they present new, challenging perspectives and ideas. They create trends and have an uncanny way of knowing what the future needs, in several professional industries. It's a gift of theirs to persist ahead of the curve and shout out their discoveries on the mountain top.

The eleventh Sign of the Zodiac can be slightly arrogant in nature and seldom believe they are wrong. Once their mind is made up, there's no reason to argue. As a matter of fact, confrontations are always a last resort for an Aquarian when proving a point. They'd rather you respect their position and leave them be. Their days are concentrated on bushwhacking new trails they can be proud of and remaining poised for the accolades they know they'll receive at a later date. Bold, yet highly intelligent, imaginative, yet pensive enough to plan, Aquarius are the perfect combination of wild and thoughtful, always rooting for the underdog, and supporting ingenuity from the most unlikely places. I've had some unique, Aquarian experiences in my life, but none can compare to the time I worked with the most beautiful alien I've ever met.

Like most teenagers, I had one of my first jobs at a supermarket in Yonkers, NY.

Shop-Rite was a major grocery store chain in the heart of the city, and many nationalities shopped and worked there. I loved working in an establishment where I could talk to different types of people. The job afforded me a chance to learn varied perspectives of a person and appreciate people regardless of their backgrounds.

There was a young lady I used to work with named Amy. She was a Caucasian, 15-year old that stood 5 feet 4 inches tall. She simultaneously rocked blue, red, yellow, and purple streaks in her hair. Amy was very thin and wiry in disposition, and everyone at my job made fun of her. My co-worker loved punk rock not hip hop, smoked Marlboros not Newport's, wore rundown black leather boots not shell-topped Adidas. Amy was an outcast in the store, and a constant target for jokes by insensitive youngsters. I loved her seemingly unconventional ways. She was a unique person who cared little about others opinion of her. I admired how, despite the mean taunts she received on a daily basis, she walked proudly in her skin and seemed unphased by people's narrow-minded behavior. It was always fun when our manager would place us on registers next to one another. Amy would make me laugh hysterically with comments made under her breath for my ears only. She would sing songs no one knew to customers that didn't care. She would create on-the-spot poems about the food items purchased by a customer on her line. Amy was pure comedy, and I adored her. One day, as she was scanning a customer's groceries, we began a running joke that lasted for months. It followed up with a skit that would irritate most people but made my side split with laughter. Out of the blue, I would ask, "Hey, Amy what time is it?" and she immediately would retort with a reference to a Beastie Boys song, "What time is it, Sonja? IT'S TIME TO GET ILL!"

She would create a frenzy of food flying across the bar code scanners, attempting to pick up the price of an item but more concentrated on the speed in which she tossed it. Cookies, juices, apples, and soup would go flying down the conveyor belt, leaving the customer hollering for a manager for assistance because she was haphazardly "manhandling" their groceries. It was an annoying, teenage stunt that would leave us in tears every time. The manger never caught her, and she'd deny her involvement if anyone complained. What a riot Amy was! I admired her wit, and gumption to be original. She taught me about the freedom and necessity to live out loud!

What would the world be like if everyone felt "free to be"? What if we concentrated on respect more than rules, and care rather than control? I suspect there would be a continuous interest in our neighborhoods based on intrigue and wonder rather than fear, paranoia, and assumptions. Aquarian energy is certainly an advocate for this utopia. The love of humanity is a gift it wishes to share. It sits in quiet agony watching senseless wars, homeless children, the abuse of elders, and animals becoming extinct at an alarming rate. The Water Bearer believes we are all each other's keeper and wishes that mankind as a whole could see our positive evolution is dependent on knowledge and support of one another. To the Aquarian, you are less than credible if your only intent behind a charitable act focuses on the tax write off, or an opportunity to brag at a cocktail party about your superficial contribution. They become annoyed when other signs shy away from a humane responsibility, believing we have to do our part and save the world. This way of life for Aquarius stems from the belief that human beings are the most intelligent animals on the planet Earth, and we should utilize our resources to sustain harmony and experience less confrontation. In the mind of an Aquarian, why fight the flow of nature? Facilitate its growth by assisting with the inevitable progression of human development. They are one of the few signs in the zodiac with the ability to remain emotionally detached from the process. They see the plight of humanity as a duty, not an arduous task. Aquarius energy rolls up its sleeves, and dives in a project headfirst. The freedom-seeking confidence they possess always garners a solution to the collective problems we share.

I recently fell in love with the humanitarian efforts of Michael Holston aka "The Real Tarzan". He is a twenty-something year old, Black man residing in Miami, FL. His life's mission is to bring balance to our planet's ecosystem by rescuing endangered animals. Michael unabashedly challenges local and national governments on their lack of interest and investment in saving the animal kingdom. He has been recognized for putting major attention on ivory pillaging from elephants, removing debris from the shells of sea turtles, and assisting wildlife rescue centers with clean up and maintenance of beaches worldwide. This young man's purpose is clear, and no one will prevent him from restoring harmony to our planet.

The Real Tarzan marches into remote jungles, with "balls of steel", looking for the most exotic snakes in an effort to relocate them. This keeps the snakes from being hunted by corporations who wish to make rare handbags to sell for thousands of dollars. He intuitively converses with apes and chimpanzees, as if they were his childhood friends, anticipating their responses and playfully escorting them in the hands of scientists who wish to study their environment and keep them safe from mass extermination. Michael is a godsend that needs to be recognized and supported, rather than ridiculed. Most recently, he and his team were threatened by law officials in Miami for rescuing iguanas. Apparently, the sea level has risen on the southern coast of Florida causing thousands of land animals to drown or be captured by local hunters and killed. Michael and his team travelled in the dead of the night to rescue these beautiful reptiles from trees, under rocks, and swamplands, and relocated them to other coastal habitats in Florida or rescue centers that would care for them. He was cited by local authorities for improperly relocating wild animals. When in fact, they intended to sell these animals elsewhere for their own gain. Even though these charges were far from the truth, they continued to harass Mike and his crew for interfering with "police work". Michael's argument was that you cannot ransack an environment with a short-sighted plan. In his eyes, authorities have been contributing the imbalance of the planet, due to global warming, by exterminating anything that gets in their way. The Real Tarzan passionately explains the need to bring balance and restoration by coming together, as a human race, with compassion and respect for all living things. These seemingly Aquarian undertakings make him a hero in my heart, and a necessary citizen of the world. Many people are full of complaints, only to add to a selfish society that forces us all to the brink of extinction; Michael Holston is actually putting drive behind a purpose and doing something about it.

Everyone can benefit from utilizing the energy Aquarians naturally possess. Every sign is activated within us, in some area of our lives, and the Water Bearer teaches us to pay closer attention to the well-being of people other than ourselves. It's a gift of theirs to recognize the needs of another, and find the most efficient, sensible way to assist in their growth and happiness. This quality is what makes them one of the best friends you'll ever have. Aquarius people are considerate and understanding to those they truly care about. They are honest with their opinion, yet supportive of whatever crazy idea their friend harbors. Their emotionally detached disposition has an advantageous quality, as well. Void of possessiveness, many feel free to relate to Aquarians because they stand clear of being overly dramatic, nor do they take too much to heart. Always giving their buddies freedom to be unconventional allows trust, honesty, and vulnerability to flourish in their relationships. Aquarius are the biggest supporters and encouragers. Friendships are a chosen family, and they couldn't be prouder of their tribe. They enjoy sharing ideas and resources. Aquarians can be quite loquacious, and are always up for mindless, superficial chatter to take the edge off an emotional day. Great listeners, and often avid readers, they have an extraordinary propensity to store loads of information akin to a computer. They have the ability to regurgitate a wide variety of facts. Forever known as the pal with the solution, Aquarians are the constant "go to" friend. They are very likeable, approachable, and super accommodating; however, you must be chosen. This air sign creates friendships they support, but they do not share information with everyone. Aquarius people are extremely motivated to only invite people in their close quarters that add value to their drama-free zone. If you are elected to share intimate space with them, consider yourself "beyond" lucky.

In the early fall of 1992, I moved to Los Angeles, California to start a new life. Initially I lived with my sweet cousin, Regina. She and her friends opened me up to a world of tacos and fresh fruit on the corner, beach life, and wide-eyed comrades willing to hustle for a life they only dreamed; amidst the Hollywood entertainment industry. Regina made me feel welcomed and supported, knowing I always needed family to fall back on in times of homesickness. Several years later, she got married, had two kids, and decided to move back to the East coast to be better supported by her and her new husband's immediate family. Although I understood her reasoning, it broke my heart to see her go. She provided a sense of comfort that I heavily relied on. She provided a sense of normalcy in a city that cared very little about my well-being. I was soon forced to discover a tribe I could trust and build lasting memories with.

The vast land mass of Greater Los Angeles threatens to swallow the dreams of any hopeful young adult. There are many ways to get distracted and thrown off course, without a solid familial structure to hold you in place. I periodically thought about moving back to New York, but quickly realized I would have to start over again in an area too cold for my liking. So, I stayed. The only way I saw fit was to make a few beautiful people my family. I socialized more with folks I worked with, organized small gatherings at my new apartment, and began sharing my poetry at local coffee houses and eateries. I stumbled across a family/friend community that warmed my soul and cultivated my love for words. The World Stage is an artist community that still resides in the culturally enriched neighborhood of Leimert Park. This predominant African American section of Central Los Angeles became my hub for good food, cultural events and festivals, private parties, and Wednesday night poetry readings. I was groomed and nurtured by elders, such as V. Kali and Kamau Daaood; well-known writers and wisdom providers still gracing the stage to this day. Besides sharing my literary work, I poured my love into those in my new circles. I was adamant to find good friends, so I had to become one. Countless dinners, gatherings, museum outings, and hair braiding sessions began to be a big part of my life. My newfound family and I shared secrets and big picture goals. At one point, a group of us beautiful women formulated a poetry collective entitled SEVEN. We broke away, slightly, from the public share at The World Stage, and created a more intimate clan of literary brilliance that further grew us. As we delved deeper into the value of our sisterhood and intimate connections through our shared poetry, I had forgotten about any plans to move home. We created a social circle that surpassed my dreams of living in Los Angeles. Not only were they family, SEVEN and the phenomenal talent of The World Stage set me on a trajectory in my life I'm extremely proud of. I chose a family that spoke to my heart and soul, talents and desires, courage and my fears. Currently, you will still find literary masters of The World Stage on Degnan Boulevard in Leimert. The societal threat of gentrification wants to push them out, however, the joy and cultural education will never be erased from the minds of those that graced the stage. It's a family connection we somehow all chose and will continue for years to come.

The universal gifts of Aquarian energy astound me. They hope to propel far past what the eyes can capture, and the heart could ever experience.

Aquarians see the world as a playground, and the future as endless possibilities. Specialized groups, lasting friendships, and useful information aid in their share. Just give them space and permission to fly and watch a eutopia of connectedness and originality develop before your very eyes.

Questions to ask the Aquarius in You:

What aspects of your life would you like to be remembered for your unique standpoint?

How can you better serve the planet, or your neighbor, from a selfless perspective?

How many times a day do you use a boost of "over confidence", or borderline arrogance, in order to secure an opportunity, you may not be ready for?

Can you give equal attention to your intimate relationships and business/distant relationships, simultaneously?

Haniel's Corner:

Dear Aquarius, you have been called to usher practical people and situations in a cosmic direction. You show a growing need for a world that understands astrology, the metaphysical, the unusual, and the plight of mankind. Many may not understand your vision, but that's not your concern. Use the delightful side of your confidence to prove the impossible and show credence to the unbelieving. Your reasoning and charm show the world that anything is possible. Your detached emotions allow you to keep everything in perspective, while gleefully expressing differences in a convincing way. You are the gatekeeper between the heavens and the earth, and the intelligent imagination that is decisive and determined enough to make sure every voice is heard. Remain open to a world that would rather create solo missions. You are the glue that makes it all make sense.

Mantra:

"I am open to receive the knowledge, love, and support from unfamiliar sources, even when I think I know it all!"

CHAPTER TWELVE

꯭

PISCES – The Wise One

"Human beings are boring and predictable.
I see their true intentions beyond what they show.
Absorbing everyone's madness through unconditional love;
keeping the PEACE, is all I know!"

There's a subtle power proposed by the act of compassion. It sneaks into the crevices of your soul with the intention of loving another in places unobvious to most. This warmth is unassuming, yet tenacious, soft, alluring, overlooked (at times), and absolutely necessary. The life of a tender soul, in a world that would rather you swallow you whole, can be a complicated one. However, if anyone can live it, the peaceful spirit of Pisces the Fish has a chance. The final incarnation of the zodiac shows the importance of putting yourself completely in another's shoes, feeling the world's joys and sorrows in an effort to remember we are all one race, one nation, and one miracle of God. This pliable water sign often sacrifices its own needs to pay reverence to others. They intrinsically know that the act of giving is a cyclical process, and when they show love, love will find its way to them. In this way, Pisces energy appears to be naïve, but nothing could be further from the truth. Their actions are intentional. A simple and easy approach to life produces far better results than asserting control to meet demands. According to them, it's a noble gesture to surrender to aggressive people by applying understanding and sensitivity in combative situations. An overexcited ego is a waste of time and energy. Besides, in their own way, be it passive aggressive, they discover ways to get what they want. The wisdom of Pisces people is difficult for a "power hungry" society to comprehend. They believe in the power of love and the acceptance that everything happens at the right time. It gives their surroundings permission "to be", without judgement or criticism. This outlook allows them to engage the harsh realities of life by coating every challenge with hope and possibilities. Control is a figment of their imagination, and mercy is a law to live by. I've been a beneficiary to Pisces' form of surrender. It teaches you that time is an illusion, and we are always in the right place, at the right time.

During a very pivotal point in my life, I met Akahdahmah, a dear soul-mate. It seemed he appeared out of nowhere as a promise from God, and a saving gesture from my ancestors. When I was released from my recording contract with LaFace Records in 1995, I was approaching my one-year residency in Atlanta, GA. I originally moved there to be closer to the record labels headquarters, in an effort to gain a better rapport with the company's department heads. It seemed like a smart move at the time, in effort to get to know the marketing and publicity executives more personally in hopes they could better promote my album once it was released. Although I was able to initiate a few lasting friendships and become a more well-rounded artist by engaging in some dynamic live music sets, I hated living in the south. It was entirely too slow for this city slicker. Everyone seemed to be a "big fish in a little pond" and relished the idea of making themselves more important than their efforts or accolades suggested. I was over the small-town competition, and desperately wanted to move back to Los Angeles.

After a three week visit to LA, I asked the friends I was vacationing with if they would mind if I moved in with them. They did. Suggesting, in so many words, my welcome had been worn; now what was I going to do? Atlanta was not an option, and I virtually had no money after my small recording advance from LaFace.

About two days before I decided to go back to Georgia to figure it all out, I met a tattoo artist named Pedro Balugo (God bless his soul), who gave me a sweet deal on my first tattoo: $20 for an Egyptian rune called Wunjo, located at the top of my spine, that translates to mean, "joy and light". I was stoked! Pedro was well respected, and one of the coolest Sagittarians you'd ever meet. While we conducted this life-altering, permanent event, somewhere between pain and amazement, Akahdahmah walked through the front door.

He smelled like prosperity. A combination of a morning forest, geranium oil, and Nag Champa incense. He had dread locs down his back, a full beard that covered the majority of his face, and he spoke in a familiar yet endearing New Jersey accent. I knew, at that moment, I found the brother I never had. Akah represented a world I needed to live in, a community in which I could find the reflection of my heartbeat, and a refuge from the selfish, competitive world of the music industry. Within the initial hour of us meeting, we laughed and discovered a similar interest in music and need to redirect our lives for Spirit (God) through rituals, natural living, and a fondness for herbal remedies. Akah was a clear vision of a street I wanted to travel down. His presence seems to create opportunities to help realign my soul and my priorities. I explained to him my desire to move back to Los Angeles, and how I didn't have a place to say. Without missing a beat, and within two hours of knowing each other, he offered his place for me to crash until I emerged on my feet. With a quickness, I agreed. It sounds crazy, and downright dangerous, but there was a knowing deep in my heart that we were supposed to be in each other's lives. Akah's offering didn't appear as a sexual advance, or dangerous in nature, by any means. It felt like the divine compassion issued by the Pisces energy we are all privy to. It smacked me in my face as unconditional love, and an understanding two strangers had on a path that now required trust; a blind walk into a way of life that defied reasoning but reflected God. As we planned our new co-habitant living arrangement over the next few weeks, the New Yorker in me looked for red flags, but there were none to be found. Everyone in my life thought I was crazy and desperate. However, nothing could have felt more aligned. After eight years of living together, him getting married with one child, and me following suit; we remain family. Our relationship has been twenty-five years in the making, and still going strong. Other than my mother and my son, there's no one on the planet I feel closest to. He retrieved me from a heap of madness, on the heels of an interesting ride. Our connection displayed an emotional intelligence I haven't experienced since.

There's a certain kind of genius displayed within a Pisces' psyche. They quickly assess their environment with an incredible intuitive awareness that stuns the rational thinking of most people. It's like the pieces of a puzzle join together in their minds, and they consciously know what is right for any situation. These considerate creatures are sometimes drawn to the complexities of mathematics and art. They enjoy following the steps of numbers and equations, and the possible reward for their diligence at the end of their discoveries. Artistic endeavors explore the imagination that stems past what's visible to the world. They bend concepts in music and visual arts into stories the common person has a difficult time comprehending. Pisces energy extends reality and takes various risks in expression, so we may feel what they feel. This heightened sense of intelligence cheapens with explanation; you just have to experience it. Unlike Aquarians, Pisces people do not boast about how smart they are. They humbly accept that information comes to them fluidly, and quite magically. They unconsciously rely on the ethereal power of Angels, Guides, and most things unseen. Whether you believe in the presence of Spirits and Ancestors is not important to them; most Pisces are conscious of the fact that they always feel a presence or a knowing that's bigger than them. This allows them to tap into an existence beyond what the physical world can prove. Akin to taking the same ingredients we all use in making a cake and adding unlikely additions such as pepper and honey... viola! You have the most delicious cake you've ever tasted, inspired by an imagination that was bold enough to trust itself. Piscean willingness to accept this creative curiosity adds to their genius. By allowing an inherent knowing and innate intuition to lead the way, they are capable of completing any and all impossible task.

Quincy Jones is a widely recognized Pisces. He's also been credited as an outstanding record producer, multi-instrumentalist, songwriter, composer, arranger, and film and television producer. His history in the music industry spans over six decades, highlighting a plethora of accomplishments ranging from his 28 Grammy awards to producing the most noted and uber popular album, "Thriller", by Michael Jackson, which sold over 80 million copies worldwide. If you are ever so privileged to watch footage of him working and creating music, you will be amazed at the concentration he displays within his creative process. It's like watching a human computer pulling information out of the sky and assigning the urges he receives to designated instruments. This tenuous connection has left many of his peers astonished and bewildered by the hundreds of thousands of formulas and equations he has conjured up to support his varied imagination. Over the six decades of work, he has managed to take the same twelve, standard notes and adjust them in ways that sound new and improved each time; that is pure genius! Using the same twelve notes is a challenge some of the greatest musicians alive couldn't fathom. Also, take into account that he has successfully remained relevant throughout many incarnations of musical genres and tastes.

"The Wiz" soundtrack/score was one of his most influential projects, as a music and film producer. This African American offshoot of the "The Wizard of Oz" has become a cult classic among millions of Black patrons, and inspired artists starting from its release in 1978.

The musical starred Michael Jackson, Diana Ross, Nipsey Russel, and Ted Ross, just to name a few. Although the movie opened to mediocre reviews, due to its low budget and poor marketing, Quincy Jones was able to energize a slew of hopeful entertainers with his soulful rendition of the classic story line. Mr. Jones' music highlighted exceptional rhythmic patterns, heartfelt stories, and customized arrangements for every vocalist hired. His genius allowed him to not only pull from the inspiration of the specific talent he directed, but also thrust forward a sound he wanted people to consider. In his fluid, shape shifting Pisces way, he was able to intuitively connect with what our culture needed then and now. "The Wiz" and his many other creations are timeless. His creativity was, and still is, finding a plausible way to reach the heart and soul with music, in a way that speaks emotion and subtle class to every person within earshot. He is truly tapped into a spiritual rapture beyond time and space.

The sensitivity of Pisces energy goes beyond the grasp other zodiac signs can achieve. It has the arduous task of absorbing, and often retaining, the feelings of the world. Pisces are able to sense unspoken anger from their spouse, frustration from a stranger in a local supermarket, or sadness from a father on the news who just lost their sibling to an accident. This quick assimilation of energy is initiated by a fierce sympathy for all living creatures. Pisces people have a difficult time experiencing the suffering of another. So, they willingly and subconsciously absorb it as their own. They instantly become involved with who, what, and where another's pain stems from, out of a need to identify with and rectify a situation, so harmony may ensue as quickly as possible. Many days, they walk around laden with another's madness unable to decipher if it's their emotions they're responsible for addressing, or the feelings of another. It's a powerful gift to act as the cleaner of energy, and the remover of all unwanted sensations on the planet. However, the wisdom to ascertain that it is simply "their duty and purpose" helps them to push through the task. Taking on this responsibility reminds me of an elder carefully cradling a baby, aware of their frailty, yet understanding that no one can handle something so delicate with as much reverence and joy as they can.

Pisces people must remember to cleanse their bodies often by large bodies of water, and with spiritual rituals, music, and quiet moments alone. These practices allow them to restore their mind, bodies, and souls. Realigning their personal energy is, yet, another task. If they lack this discipline, they may be prone to illness easier than most, or lean into addiction of some sort to numb the pain they feel. What a blessing, as the zodiac senior, to be able to care for us so openly and lovingly. With the universal love Pisces energy displays, we couldn't be in better hands. The energy I attempt to create, with the help of my staff at certain events, is akin to Pisces energy; an open acceptance of love that teaches us all how to trust the heart of another.

Our Wordlife Astrology Retreats are becoming increasingly popular. For the past three years, we have gathered in the magical presence of Sedona, AZ. This red rock terrain is nestled quietly between Phoenix and Flagstaff and showcases several vortexes (energy surges) that stretch from the center of the earth to the universe. These vortexes promote several energetic shifts within a person when they're dosed in them. Suddenly, you're thinking becomes clear; you may sleep more often than usual; you may eat, cry, or become more creative than you expect. These energetic forces help to align your mind, body, and spirit in unexpected ways, however, always purposeful and healing by nature.

When we assemble, a few classes and workshops are offered to teach and inform, such as Western Astrology, womb awareness for women, Ayurvedic medicine, and yoga. We focus on self-healing and emptying out pain that no longer serves us. One year, we participated in an exercise that encouraged us to face those who have wronged us in the past. We courageously called out the accusers of our childhood pain and trauma, in order to identify what we were holding onto and forgive all involved. Many of the retreat attendees enlisted the osmosis technique of a Pisces and became sick due to the sadness and pain they were absorbing. Memories and recollections of certain instances began to pour out into the room, with nothing to hold onto. Emotional energy, like sound and light waves, may not be visible to the naked eye, but is very real and must attach itself to a host to feed off of. We weren't prepared for such an emotional eruption of sorts, and some were left to hold anguish for others. We quickly used spiritual tools such as sage, sound vibrations, and prayers to usher unwanted energy off of those involved. We ventured outside to let nature step in and cleanse unseen areas. We drank copious amounts of water and released whatever we could. It was surprising for some. Many are not used to the shared responsibilities of such emotional alterations within the body that Pisces people partake in on a daily basis. However, we proudly got through it, knowing we felt stronger together. The wisdom of unconditional love carried us through the rest of our retreat. It's in the top three reasons why people have decided to return; a bond and deep connection are always made, assuring trust and true compassion for our brothers and sisters on the planet.

A Pisces' responsibility to love with their mind, body and soul is a thankless existence, at best. Many plow through life eager to obtain riches and notoriety. Beneficial as they may be, Pisces energy takes care of what often goes unnoticed. Unlimited care, concern, understanding, and gentleness are ways to help sustain happiness and ease in another's life. Their sometimes spacey and idealistic approach is necessary, in order to protect themselves from the harshness of reality. Imagination keeps them detached from unnecessary pain and egotistical glory.

Pisces has a wisdom that's becoming increasingly more necessary in our society. Its energy reminds us that the power of the unseen is more powerful than material gain. It recognizes a source bigger than us always giving directions to pursue our highest good. Call it God, Jehovah, whatever title you'd like, Pisces' job is to remind us of the power of the unknown and its inevitable power. It's the last incarnation of the zodiac, suggesting energy turned into personality characteristics via Western Astrology, and a beginning to what has yet to be discovered. There's honor in the inevitable evolution of Pisces energy.

Questions to ask the Pisces in You

How are you emotionally responsible for your fellow man or woman?

Do you walk through life selfishly concerned with only your advancements, without considering the concerns of the collective?

Do you find ways to escape reality, more than often, with substances that temporarily dull your senses?

Do you notice spirits, or sense a presence that's not visible? Do you ask what it wants, or do you run from it, feeling a lack of control?

Haniel's Corner:

Dear Pisces, never cower from those who don't understand your spiritual acuity. You are more dynamic than most. You're a courageous, wise spirit, in a land of "babies", and that is not an easy feat. You must teach the rest of us the power of love and selflessness. Mistakes emerge largely due to your efforts to assimilate to the mass majority and their impressions of you. You become passive aggressive and self-sabotaging, in an effort to gain their respect. Obtain the highest expression of yourself by believing in your magic and watch everyone come to you. Proving yourself and over-explaining your genius deplete your energy. Find confidence in being the best you can be with what God has given you. You are a tremendous gift to behold!

Mantra:

"I am courageous enough to integrate the power of the Divine with the practical and realistic needs of the planet."

YOUR TESTIMONIES : MY REFLECTIONS

I am overwhelmed with gratitude!

"I stumbled across one of your sessions on Instagram in 2016 or 2017 (whenever the Solar Eclipse in Leo happened), anyway you did a live reading for me (Leo-Sun, Cap-Moon, Gem- Rise) and during the reading you mentioned that I felt "Crispy" or "Crunchy" to you. At the time you said it, I didn't think much of it other than you alluding to the fact that at the time I was not a water drinker. Fast forward to 2019 and I wind up having 16 inches of my Large Intestines removed due to numerous "Diverticula". In my heart I know that had I listened to you at that time it's highly likely that the situation could have been avoided. Needless to say, I've been water siphon ever since and I try to never miss a YouTube broadcast.

On another note, I want to thank you for your generosity and compassion. God has a way of showing the world who people really are and your light shines from your face like a beacon of love! Thank you, beautiful soul!"

DeAnna Brown
Leo

"My experience with Sonja Marie has been God sent. I ran into her on Facebook for her Weekly Rundown during a time in my life when questions surrounded me with no answers. Through her online forum, "The Village", as we are affectionately called, we share and learn and grow together. My experience with the Village led me to get a reading which I discovered fear, kept me from facing some hard truths about myself. Through God, my Spirit Angels and Guides, Sonja Marie and the Village, I am healing old wounds and look forward to continuing to evolve into a better version of myself. All your questions will be answered when you are ready to receive them. When Sonja popped up on my timeline, I was ready, and the journey began.

Thank u! Forever grateful."
D Stokes
Taurus

"I am so honored and privileged to be a part of the Village. Sonja has a way of teaching astrology in a way that is easy to understand. Her wealth of knowledge combined with her poetic visuals and NY swag makes her the perfect person to get a message across to any generation. I appreciate her so much."

Victoria
Scorpio

"I was introduced to Sonja Marie about five years ago from a friend on Periscope; I didn't know what I was in for. One day, I asked for a free, public reading and sent my birth information. I was driving while listening to her reading my specific natal chart. I pulled my car over in tears of excitement that someone could see me and know me deeply without ever talking to me. I knew she was connected; most definitely! That's where our relationship began. I started making her weekly rundowns a priority in my life. Sonja Marie's gift of teaching is a blessing to my personal journey of healing myself from the inside/out. There were times when I wanted to have a pity party and she coached me into understanding where that behavior came from and gave me tools - spiritually and astrologically - to help serve my inner work. With that being said, if you ever get an opportunity to work with Sonja Marie it's a blessing to your life. She will guide you to self-mastery if you're willing to do the work. It will be uncomfortable, but very rewarding."

Tatianna Thompson
Aries

"My Astro/Spiritual reading with Sonja Marie was such a wonderful blessing and experience. She is a vessel of light, love and Spirit! It actually was so much more than I could have ever expected. During our call I was blessed with the confirmation that my Ancestors are very much present in my life. I was given tools to unlock blockages to my path of growth and freedom! It was very much a spiritual experience!"

Tion D
Taurus

"The ability to take broad concepts and be able to apply them in one's daily reality is key to embracing any spiritual or philosophical practice. Sonja Marie has been able to speak to me in a language that I am open to and can fully understand. Her down to earth approach makes astrology accessible even when she is discussing layered and sometimes complex concepts."

Tenjin Ikeda
Scorpio

"SQUIRREL! :0) So many gifts from Spirit this beautiful lady has given me in The Village and in readings. I never considered the perfection that Yonkers & Spirit could make, but she's here! Uniquely gifted and giving."

Nicole B.
Aries

"I never thought my healing would take place through astrology and then I met Sonja Marie...my life has never been the same! I thank you!"

Lucy Taylor
Aquarius

You gave me a quick read on Periscope on a Friday in November 2017..... and girl, you READ me, and I did NOT want to hear it, but it was soooooo useful. These last three years I have grown so much and taken your advice and I now understand what I couldn't understand then.

Britney Wade
Pisces

You so cute. We love you. I sent my whole family to you & I don't play about my family.

Thembi
Aries

I LOVE Sonja Marie for so many reasons. On the surface, she's cute, bubbly, and jam packed with a lot of knowledge that she gracefully shares. Getting to the root of who Sonja is and really connecting with her, is having a reading with her. Sonja tells it like it is, very blunt, and to the point! Doing the spiritual work, and consistently in tune with her weekly live check-ins, confirmation led me to take what she said to me in that reading, apply it, and begin to heal. Thank you, Sonja Marie for being a vessel to receive the message I needed for healing on my spiritual journey.

Mena Love
Cancer

My experience with Sonja Marie was authentic and literally, lifesaving. I had a reading in which my adherence/obedience to messages presented by my Guides, had me walk more lovingly. Employing a more loving state of mind, in a timely fashion; saved a loved one's life THE-VERY-NEXT-DAY! Sonja Marie is a brilliant conduit of light.

Shree Turner-Sophas
Aries

I loved getting a mother/daughter reading from Sonja. What I loved even more was gifting one to my sister and seeing the contrast that the stars provided! Oh, and my ancestors came through!!! So cool! She's the real deal! Oh, and the retreats?... OMG!

Kimani
Gemini

Sonja Marie opened my thinking up to a whole new world of intuition, thought, power, and vibration. Her practical way of mapping through Western Astrology helped to positively redirect my action and thoughts about life and finding a balance that works for me.

Asa Lovechild Arnold
Taurus

Upon our first introduction, Sonja mentally teleported for about 45 secs then returned back on the beat. It was like being in a movie; I thought "Wow, she's super cool".

Katrina L.
Leo

I became acquainted with Sonja Marie and her work through Wordlife Astrology quite by accident. A Facebook announcement that her Astrology 101 class was being offered in Oakland where I live, piqued my interest and I attended the workshop. Sonja Marie has a unique gift for making a complex and often daunting system accessible for newbies and more advanced students, alike. Over the years the use of her intuitive learning approach to understanding Western Astrology has enriched both the lives of myself and my family. My son and I had a parent/child reading with Sonja Marie a few years ago, the information came through that he came back for me, as well as an admonition to watch his health. Both insights were well-founded and have helped deepen our connection. This year I gave my husband a reading with her for his birthday. He was reluctant, but afterward shared that it was powerful, everything she said was spot on, and that it was his favorite thing he'd done all year! I'm grateful for Sonja Marie and the ever-deepening understanding of myself and the world that I have gained from her online offerings, readings, and in-person retreats.

Jeannine Hooks-Allen
Aquarius

So here I am! Signed up for an astrology/reading workshop by my best friend who never showed up. And I was forced to experience Sonja all by myself!

I had no idea what to expect.

Here I was, raw as I can be, open with my birthdate, the time I was born and where I was born.

Sonja is so real, that it will scare the shit out of you. Her authenticity ripped my heart apart by what was said!

Since that day, I was blessed by her guidance, light, and wisdom but most of everything our friendship and sisterhood.

Sister of my heart, I acknowledge every word of guidance she gives me.

Witnessing her spreading her light and empowering each one of us is a gift I am always grateful.

Sandrine K.
Pisces